THE JONAH JOURNEY

FROM DISOBEDIENCE TO DESTINATION

BY DAVID JONES

LUCIDBOOKS

This book is dedicated to my Lord and Savior, Jesus Christ! Without You, I would not have been able to do this. Thank You for being my courage and my words to write this book. My prayer is that it blesses everyone who reads it and that it makes a powerful impact for Your kingdom that is to come.

To my wife Tonia, and my sons, Jeremiah, and Micah, thank you for your love, support, and encouragement along this spiritual journey. I thank God for you each and every day that I bow my head and pray. I love you all with the fullness of my heart!

TABLE OF CONTENTS

INTRODUCTION

1 Samuel 15:22-23 says, "Look: to obey is better than sacrifice, to pay attention is better than the fat of rams. For rebellion is like the sin of divination, and defiance is like wickedness and idolatry." Obedience is, indeed, better than sacrifice. I know this personally, and God has taken my misery and has turned it into motivation for writing this book.

I experienced my own personal "Jonah Journey" when I decided to go against God's counsel and left the job where I had been working for almost 11 years. I had become stagnant, and I truly felt like I was just wasting my time because nothing fruitful was coming out of it. I had even got passed over for a promotion, only to watch it be given to someone who was very unqualified and didn't even have the years of experience that I had. In my mind, it was time to go. It was time to find something else that was more suitable and adventurous.

I applied to various opportunities but never got any responses for interviews. The day came when I finally got a response. I was excited, and I started praying to God that if this was a good opportunity for me, He would bless me to transition into it.

As I was sitting in the final meeting with the manager for the new position, she informed me of the starting pay. God had answered my prayer and was letting me know that this wasn't for me, because my current position paid more. I could hear God speaking to me saying, "David, do not take this job. You are fine where you are, and I have a plan for you if you will just wait on Me."

I was so ready for a change of direction, that I foolishly accepted the position. God had actually presented me with an opportunity to take a course to get a certificate to be a paralegal, but instead, I chose to run...run down my own path of disobedience. What I did not realize was that I was about to embark on a journey that was going to leave me as a helpless hinderance to my wife, Tonia.

Throughout this book, I will be taking you along on my journey of disobedience that I like to call "The Jonah Journey." I will also be diving into the book of Jonah on his journey to see the consequences of his actions and how they relate to us today. I pray that my testimony and the story of Jonah inspires you, but above all, encourages you to seek God, no matter how far you've gone in the wrong direction. God bless you and thank you for purchasing this book!

CHAPTER 1
DESTINED FOR YOUR DESTINATION

I have good news and bad news. The good news is, God has an orchestrated plan for all of our lives. The bad news is, most of the time, we don't know what it is, and when we finally discover it, it doesn't match up with the ideas and plans we have in mind. We are created with a purpose. God is calling us to go somewhere and to be somebody in order to represent Him and His kingdom that is to come. The amazing thing is God didn't just decide to give us a plan and a purpose yesterday. He established it before we were even born! Jeremiah 1:5 says, "I chose you before I formed you in the womb; I set you apart before you were born. I appointed you a prophet to the nations."

If you are like me, I'm sure you have asked God on several occasions what your purpose is and what does His plan for your life entail. One thing I have discovered is that in order to reach your destination (the prepared places and positions produced by God), you must go on a journey. The journey is the reason why God doesn't always tell us, up front, who we are and where we are going. The journey prepares us for our destination. If God told us everything He had planned for us, we would probably disagree and proceed to tell Him what our future is supposed to look like.

The journey does three things while we are en route to our destination: It breaks us down, it builds us up, and it brings us in. The breakdown occurs when we let go of ourselves, our plans, and purposes in order to get on God's agenda. This part of the journey is tough because, sometimes, it's hard to let go of your dreams and your plans, especially when you realize it's not what God has in store for you. You might have plans to become a doctor or a lawyer, but God's plans might be for you to pastor a church. You might be content in the city where you live because you know everybody, and you know where everything is. God might be calling you to relocate to a new geographical area so that He can use you in a more fulfilling way for ministry. The breakdown occurs once you realize God has made His plans clear to you. The length of the breakdown depends on you and how long you choose to wrestle with God.

After the breakdown, we experience the buildup. This is when we have surrendered everything, and we are willing to follow God's plan. We don't do it begrudgingly, we do it with peace in knowing that God knows best. Whatever He chooses to do, we believe it will be for our good and for His glory. This part of the journey is where we grow more in our faith as God continues to prepare us for our destination. We learn to depend more on Him and less on ourselves and our abilities.

The final step of the journey is when we are brought in. God brings us into the plans and purposes that He has established for us. In other words, we reach our destination! Once we arrive, we are well prepared and carry a testimony about the journey we went on to get there. It is always inspiring to hear people testify about going one way in their lives, only to see God show up and send them in a new direction. God has given us such testimonies to read about in the Bible:

Abraham was a man living an ordinary life, but God destined him to be the father of many nations (Genesis 17:5). His journey didn't begin until he departed from the comfortable confines of his homeland (Genesis 12:1-3). Joseph was just seventeen years old and attending to sheep (Genesis 37:2). God had destined him to be second in command over all of Egypt (Genesis 41:40-41), but his journey didn't begin until his brothers threw him in a pit and sold him into slavery (Genesis 37:24-28).

David, like Joseph, was also young and attending to sheep when God destined him to be king over Israel (1 Samuel 16:11-13). His journey to the throne didn't begin until he was commanded to move into Saul's courts for service (1 Samuel 16:21-23). We most certainly cannot forget about Paul! Paul stood by and watched Stephen, one of the first deacons of the church, get stoned to death (Acts 7:58). Paul was also a persecutor of the church (Acts 8:2-3). God had destined Paul to be the deliverer of the Gospel to the Gentiles, as well as kings and Israelites (Acts 9:15), but his journey didn't begin until he had an encounter with Jesus on the road to Damascus (Acts 9:1-9).

It doesn't matter where you are, currently, or where you have been. God knows where He wants to take you, and He knows how to get you there. It might seem like you have been trying to find your way for a long time, and maybe you are still searching, but don't miss out on the fact that you are on a journey to your destination. In Genesis 28:10-22, Jacob finds himself in a lonely place. He is on the run from his brother Esau, because he has stolen Esau's blessing and Esau wants revenge (Genesis 27). Jacob is heading to his uncle's house and stops in this place because it is getting dark.

To Jacob, this is just a place to rest his head for the night, but God visits him in a dream to let him know that this place isn't just a place of rest, it's going to be a place of residency for Jacob and his offspring. In this moment of his life, Jacob is single and doesn't have any children. God has let Jacob know that he has a future and that the ground he was sleeping on was his destination.

The next six chapters detail Jacob's journey, but in Genesis 35:1a, God fulfills His promise to Jacob: God said to Jacob, "Get up! Go to Bethel and settle there." After his dream, Jacob awoke with a faithful realization that God was surely with him and he named that place Bethel, which means "House of God." Jacob made a vow before setting out on his journey to his destination. He said "If God will be with me and watch over me during this journey I'm making, if He provides me with food to eat and clothing to wear, and if I return safely to my father's family, then the LORD will be my God' (Genesis 28:20-21).

My friend, I want you to know that God is with you as you go on your journey. I want you to know that He is going to provide for you and protect you, even when you can't see how or you can't understand what is going on. He wants to be your one and only God, and through your journey, you will get to experience Him like never before and you will realize that He is your one and only source for all that you need (Philippians 4:19).

So, what about this guy named Jonah? We've all heard the account of his story. When I was little, whenever I heard the name "Jonah," I always thought about the man getting swallowed up by the big fish. But there is so much more to Jonah's story, and when we take a closer look, we get a good look at our own lives. Jonah was destined for a destination but decided to run, and within his rebellion, we see some other issues that prevented Jonah from being obedient in the first place. As we journey through this book, we will take a closer look into Jonah and discover who he was, where he came from and the issues that he carried deep within that caused him to run from God. I will also share more of my own journey and the lessons that I learned along the way. Let's see what the journey looks like when God delivers us from our disobedience and places us at our destination!

CHAPTER 2

DISOBEDIENCE LEADS TO DETOUR

The word of the LORD came to Jonah son of Amittai: "Get up! Go to the great city of Nineveh and preach against it because their evil has come up before Me."

—Jonah 1:1-2

June 22, 2018. It was my last day on the job. Almost 11 years of service were coming to an end as I was preparing to step into a new beginning. So much love and appreciation was shown to me on that day. There was food, cards, posters, gifts, hugs, and tears as people showed how much they loved me and appreciated all that I had done for them. It was truly a blessing to see how much of an impact I had made, not just in my work, but also in people's personal lives. There were days when God would put me in place to speak uplifting words to people who were going through situations, and sometimes would give me Scriptures to share.

The celebration would be short lived because the new job was going to be the start of a downward spiral that only God could bring me out of. Everything started off well, but in a matter of time, I discovered that I had chosen a place that was full of hostility, immaturity, and at times, pushing for unethical practices just to keep the numbers going. After four months, I realized the error in my decision. I believe God even opened up a window for me to return to my previous place of employment because I ran into my former site manager, and she asked if everything was going well. My pride was too great to tell her the truth, and I didn't want to return as a failure, especially after receiving such a grand farewell.

Looking back, I should have swallowed my pride and told her the truth. I had forgotten just that quick how much I was loved and how I would have been welcomed back with open arms. God was trying to save me from the path that was starting to develop, and it wasn't going anywhere good. The weight of things had gotten too heavy, and I decided to make another crucial decision.

There is an anonymous quote that says, "Life can teach you lessons, but pride will not let you learn." God is the giver of life, and He is always dishing out teaching lessons. I was about to become a student because God was getting ready to teach me some lessons that would be painful, but yet, productive in my growth as a Christian, a man, a husband, and a dad.

LET THE JOURNEY BEGIN

Jonah is probably the most known of all the minor prophets in the Bible and he is definitely someone that we can all relate to. His story tells of a man on a mission trying to depart from God's will, and taking desperate measures in order to accomplish it. Aside from the book of Jonah, he's only mentioned a few other times. We know that his father's name was Amittai (Jonah 1:1), that he resided in the town of Gath-hepher (2 Kings 14:25), and that he was a descendant of the tribe of Zebulun (Joshua 19:10-13). Throughout my teenage and young adult years, I always assumed that Jonah was just a man minding his own business when God showed up commanding him to go and preach to people he didn't even know. The truth is that Jonah was already fulfilling his call as a prophet. He served during the reign of King Jeroboam II and even prophesied that the king would restore the borders of Israel (2 Kings 14:23-27).

Why would Jonah run from God? I'm pretty sure God gave Jonah plenty of assignments to preach and prophesy, so what made this call so different? What do you do when God gives you the call to go and serve the undeserved? On the grand scale of things, none of us are deserving of God's grace and mercy and we definitely do not qualify to receive the free gift of salvation, but yet it is given (John 3:16; Romans 10:9-10).

Those of us who walk with Christ, daily, are grateful for His grace and mercy that He extends to us (Lamentations 3:22-23). In return, God is expecting us to extend mercy and love to others, especially towards the people that we struggle to have relationships with. For some of us, it's that messy co-worker or that inconsiderate neighbor. For others, it might be a family member that just continues to revel in irresponsible behavior, leaving others to clean up the messes that they make. For Jonah, it was a nation of people who were longtime enemies of Israel: The Ninevites.

Nineveh was established by Nimrod, a descendant of Noah's son, Ham, who became powerful and was a great hunter in the sight of the Lord (Genesis 10:6-11). During the reign of King Hezekiah, the king of Assyria, Sennacherib, invaded Judah and captured it (2 Kings 18:13-18). The LORD showed up to defeat him and his army, which sent him home to Nineveh, where he would be murdered by his own sons (2 Kings 19:35-37). Nineveh would eventually be destroyed by God due to their sinfulness (Nahum Chapter 2), but God wanted to give them an opportunity for repentance, and He wanted Jonah to be the deliverer of the good news.

So why would Jonah run from God? One thing to take into account is that Jonah possibly feared for his life. Nineveh was known for its violent mistreatment and humiliation that they displayed towards other nations (Nahum 3:1-3). Jonah possibly thought that if he went, he would never return home and would surely be killed. Jonah responded with fear instead of faith and decided to flee. There are times on the journey of life, and in ministry, that we simply forget who God is and that He is always with us. If God is calling you to go somewhere and to do something, know for certain that He has anointed you to accomplish it. We focus more on the facts of the situation than focusing on our faith. The twelve spies of Israel had the promise of God given to them before they went out (Numbers 13:1-2), but because of the facts, they responded in fear instead of faith (Numbers 13:26-33). Jesus told the disciples that they were going to the other side (Mark 4:35), but because of the facts, their fear kicked in, causing them to ponder who Jesus was (Mark 4:37-41).

Jonah 1:3-Jonah got up to flee to Tarshish from the LORD's presence. He went down to Joppa and found a ship going to Tarshish. He paid the fare and went down into it to go with them to Tarshish from the LORD's presence.

Jonah was thoroughly opposed to God's calling for him to go and preach to Nineveh. In an act of rebellion, Jonah took his money and found a ship going to Tarshish, in order to flee from God and what God wanted to accomplish. Notice that Jonah went *down* to Joppa in order to get on the boat and then went *down* into the boat (Jonah 1:3). When you decide to run from God and the call He has placed on your life, you can guarantee that things are going to start going *DOWN!*

Just like Jonah knew, we know that we cannot escape from the LORD's presence. David makes that clear in Psalm 139:7-12. So why do we run from God when He is calling us? I think it's safe to say that our desire to control our own lives and determine our own destination causes us to put up a wall of defense against God when He shows up with the actual blueprint that defines our lives. We don't like the measurements of it, we don't like the cost of it, we don't like that it calls for us to go places and to deal with people that we feel are not suitable for us. In order to buy ourselves some time, we do like a toddler and try to run away from God, only to be caught before we can cover any ground. Our failed effort at buying time only buys us trouble that only God can pull us out of.

I'm reminded of a story I heard about a man that God had called to be a preacher. The man wanted no part of his calling and decided to ignore it and went on with his daily way of living. The man worked in a coal mine, and one day while on the job, he came very close to being crushed by one of the railway carts. Immediately after avoiding what could have been costly, he heard the Lord's voice, once again, telling him to go preach. He immediately left the job and went to answer the call.

One thing that we must remember is what I made mention of in the last chapter: God isn't calling us out of the blue to serve, preach, teach, relocate, etc. The call was established before we were even formed in the womb (Jeremiah 1:5). That means that God has equipped us with everything we need to fulfill our calling. Even if we feel like we aren't capable of doing what God is calling us to do, it's okay to let Him know that we are concerned. That's when we take the opportunity to ask Him to cultivate us and our abilities so that we can be all that He is calling us to be and that our impact reflects the coming of His kingdom.

Jonah missed out on something vital that God said when He called him to go preach to Nineveh: "because their evil has come up before Me" (Jonah 1:2b). God was letting Jonah know that Nineveh was on the clock, and that His destruction for them was close at hand. God was sending Jonah to be a warning to Nineveh, not a wanderer going away from them. There is always a purpose in what God is calling you to do. God could be calling you to speak to that co-worker that you think is strange, but He knows that they just need a smile and a kind word to get them through the day. God could be calling you to share your food with the homeless person you see every day because He knows the last time they had a meal was a few days ago. God uses us in various ways to meet the needs of others, but the majority of the time, our pride and selfishness gets in the way, and the opportunity to serve or minster to someone is missed.

At the moment of calling Jonah to go to Nineveh and preach, God didn't see them like Jonah saw them. God saw people in need of repentance, Jonah saw people who were vile and violent. God wants to pour out His compassion on people that are lost, but the opportunity is neglected when we are too busy criticizing instead of being considerate of their need for salvation.

Jesus said in Mark 13:10 "And it is necessary that the gospel be preached to all nations." We have an obligation to share our faith and to show the love of Christ to everyone, including those that we see as undeserving. Through the power of the Holy Spirit, we are able to extend ourselves to others beyond what we could imagine.

Jonah's fear, possibly mixed in with the frustration of God's call, sent him fleeing in the opposite direction. When God calls us to a place and a purpose that is uncomfortable, and our response is fear, it will eventually lead us to run away from God and what He has destined us to do. We see our actions as fear, but God sees it as disobedience that is leading us on a detour. If you think about detours, they can be good or they can be bad. There are days when my wife and I are on our way home and we will take a detour to catch some extra scenery. It gives us more time to enjoy the moment of riding and talking with each other. These are good detours to experience and enjoy. Then there are the unexpected detours that you encounter when you are driving down the highway, and all of a sudden, the road or a lane is closed. Now you have to make a detour, which throws you off of your route, and could possibly delay your arrival to your destination. These are the type of detours we hope to avoid, but sometimes, they are unavoidable. Life will bring its fair share of detours that will be unexpected and uncontrollable. We have the capability of causing our own detours, and we do so either out of pleasure or because of our plight.

Jonah set his own detour in motion because of the plight that was placed before him. What seemed like a properly planned escape route from his responsibility would turn out to be a powerful planned encounter with God. Be careful about the path you choose for your detour; it could be destructive for you as well as those around you.

CHAPTER 3
DETOUR LEADS TO DESTRUCTION

But the LORD threw a great wind onto the sea, and such a great storm arose on the sea that the ship threatened to break apart. The sailors were afraid, and each cried out to his god. They threw the ship's cargo into the sea to lighten the load. Meanwhile, Jonah had gone down to the lowest part of the vessel and had stretched out and fallen into a deep sleep. The captain approached him and said "What are you doing sound asleep? Get up! Call to your god. Maybe this god will consider us, and we won't perish."

—Jonah 1: 4-6

October 12, 2018.I quit my job. It had only been four months, but enough was enough. The pettiness and immaturity had taken its toll, and the final straw came when I got into a verbal altercation with the manager. The environment had become very uncomfortable and hostile.

Instead of being patient and taking the time to look for another position, or even swallowing my pride and reaching out to my old site manager, I tapped into my pride, and I quit. I felt like I was making a big move, that I was getting the upper hand and getting the victory. I had no idea how wrong I was because I was only thinking about myself in that moment and doing something spiteful to get back at the manager. I had no consideration for how such a move would impact my marriage or our finances. God had made things work for us, even with me taking a job with lesser pay. By His grace and mercy, we didn't miss paying any of our bills. Now I was going into deeper waters by quitting and assuming I could find something else right away. Tonia tried talking to me about it and was encouraging me not to quit. She told me to wait it out and start looking for something else. I wasn't having it. As Tonia likes to call it, my "foolish male pride" was cemented on my decision to quit and there was no changing my mind about it.

I might have been quitting my job, but what I didn't realize was that I had just enrolled myself into God's classroom of maturity and manhood. I was about to grow up really quick and God had some hands-on experience available to help me.

We have a nephew named Christian. Christian was on the verge of turning one years old and his mother was in the process of relocating to New Jersey. She had talked to Tonia and I about watching him for about two weeks while she went up to get settled in. We told her we would watch him so that she could do what she needed to do without having to worry about him. The week that we started watching Christian was the week following my departure from my job. The first lesson on deck was responsibility. Guess who had to watch Christian throughout the day while Tonia went to work? Me. I went from being a man working a 9-5 to being a full-time babysitter. My responsibilities no longer entailed dealing with phone calls, pitching products, or delivering interoffice mail.

My responsibilities became feeding the baby, changing the baby, bathing the baby, comforting the baby, entertaining the baby, and watching the annoying sing along cartoons day after day with the baby. God wasn't finished yet. The two weeks that Christian was supposed to be with us turned into three months. It was too cold for him to go to New Jersey and his mom had to wait to get the heat fixed in the house.

Other situations kept coming up that prevented him from going home, which meant more time for me to be a full-time babysitter. I have to be honest; my pride was hurting. I was a grown man waking up every day watching a one-year-old. I felt defeated and useless. This wasn't what I had in mind. I was supposed to be looking for a new job and getting back to work. This was my job now and there was no payment involved. Meanwhile, all of our bills were left on Tonia to pay.

This left my wife angry and beyond frustrated with me. My pride had done nothing but cause problems for us. I soon became frustrated with my own decision and the reality that I was waking up to everyday. I wanted out and I wanted to be back in a real work environment. When Christian would take his naps, I would get on the computer to apply for jobs. There were no answers, and the weight of my decision was being felt every day. My marriage felt broken, and I was desperate to make things right.

A DESTRUCTIVE IMPACT

Jonah is in full flight mode from the LORD and his call to preach to the great city of Nineveh. Jonah has boarded a boat and is now on his way to Tarshish, or so he thinks. God decides to meet Jonah out on the open sea by sending a great wind which causes a great storm. The storm is so great that it threatens to destroy the structure of the ship that Jonah is sailing on (Jonah 1:4). This storm has Jonah's name written all on it, but he isn't the only person aboard the boat. The sailors are panicking at the impact of this storm, and they even start throwing some of the cargo off to try and salvage the ship from being destroyed. Where is Jonah while this storm is raging? "Jonah had gone down to the lowest part of the vessel and had stretched out and fallen into a deep sleep" (Jonah 1:5b).

Jonah has gotten so comfortable and confident in his decision to rebel that he is able to stretch out and fall into a deep sleep. He was unaware that a storm was breaking out, which was gonna make an impact in his life as well as in the lives of the sailors who were on board. Like Jonah, I was confident in the decisions that I had made. I didn't see the storm that God was sending my way. One thing that I learned from my storm was that it wasn't there to scare me. God allowed it so that it could structure me. The storms in our lives can be painful, but they are also full of purpose. Our storms can also have a positive impact on the people who are in our vicinity. The storm was meant for Jonah, but it made a powerful impact on the sailors.

The captain of the ship finds Jonah sound asleep. He is appalled that someone could be sleeping at such a time as this. The captain commands Jonah to do two things: "Get up! Call to your god" (Jonah 1:6a)! Why would the captain tell Jonah to call to *his* god? The sailors on board were so afraid of the storm that they had all been calling on *their* gods, but apparently nothing was happening to ease the storm (Jonah 1:5a). The captain wants Jonah to call on his god because "maybe this god will consider us, and we won't perish" (Jonah 1:6b). Jonah doesn't have to call out to God. He knows that God is present, and he knows that he is the reason for the storm. The proof is made clear after the sailors cast lots to see who is to blame for their troubles. The lots fell directly on Jonah (Jonah 1:7).

I was watching a basketball game on tv, and the sideline reporter was giving a backstory on one of the coaches and how he approaches his players. If they have made a mistake and he wants to address it with them, he lets them know that he isn't calling them out, he is calling them up. He is calling them up to lead and to be better and to be more accountable in their efforts on the court. If you ever feel like the spotlight is on you, or that God is picking on you, change your perspective.

God isn't calling you out, He is calling you up! He knows that we are more than capable of achieving the plans and purposes He has destined for us. The lots fell on Jonah, not because God was calling him out. They intentionally fell on him because God was calling him up to be more accountable and to fulfill his calling, even though he was heading in the wrong direction.

Jonah takes the opportunity to step up and claim his responsibility. The sailors want to know who he is and where he is from. Jonah responds by letting them know his ethnicity and who it is that he exalts. Jonah says, "I'm a Hebrew. I worship the LORD, the God of the heavens, who made the sea and the dry land" (Jonah 1:9). In the middle of the storm raging, Jonah made it clear who it is that he worships. Even though he was in flight, he knew in whom his faith resided. When the storm is raging in your life, don't be afraid to let everyone know who the captain of your salvation is...Jesus Christ!

It was one thing to tell the sailors he was a Hebrew and to let them know that he worshipped the God of the heavens who created the land and sea. When Jonah spilled the beans and told them he was running away from God, greater fear set in for the sailors. Jonah basically tells them he is a spiritual fugitive on the run from the God who created everything and is in control of everything. The sailors were right in their response when they asked Jonah, "What is this you've done" (Jonah 1:10)? The sailors want to separate themselves from Jonah and his disobedience immediately and ask, "What should we do to you so that the sea will calm down for us" (Jonah 1:11)?

Jonah instructs the sailors to pick him up and throw him overboard. In doing so, the storm will calm down for them. Jonah tells them, "For I know that I am to blame for this great storm that is against you" (Jonah 1:12b). This request Jonah makes sounds horrible, doesn't it? A storm is raging beyond measure out on the open sea, and he wants to be thrown overboard into it. I believe the sailors tapped into their morality because, in spite of all that Jonah had revealed, they don't do what he says. They continue to put up a fruitless effort to row back to land. The sailors are being offered an opportunity to place their faith in God. If they act on Jonah's command, the storm will cease.

God isn't concerned with the facts of our situation; He is concerned with our faith in Him towards the situation. Our faith in God will always outweigh the facts of the situation. The sailors see a storm raging, their boat about to break apart, and a man telling them to throw him overboard. The act of faith they are asked to demonstrate seems cruel and inhumane. What Jonah knows, and what they don't know, is that God already has a plan. All they have to do is respond by faith.

What are the facts you are facing in your current situation? Not enough money? Not enough time? Not enough resources? Not enough faith? God already knows the facts of your situation. He wants your faith in Him to supersede the obvious, and in doing so, you will see Him move on your behalf in a mighty and miraculous way. Dreams will turn into realities, what seems too far out of reach will be brought near. God asked Abraham and Sarah a question when it came to His plan for them to have a baby in their old age: "Is anything impossible for the LORD" (Genesis 18:14)? They were looking at the facts of their old age, but God was only concerned with their faith in Him to deliver what He had promised them.

After seeing their efforts to reach the shore weren't going to happen, the sailors gave in and decided to throw Jonah overboard, only after pleading with God not to hold them accountable for Jonah's life or with shedding innocent blood (Jonah 1:14).

Their response was not out of faith, but out of fear. They had exhausted every other option and decided to try throwing Jonah overboard to see if it would really settle the storm (Jonah 1:15). To their surprise, the storm immediately stopped raging and "the men were seized by great fear of the LORD, and they offered a sacrifice to the LORD and made vows" (Jonah 1:16). Jonah's disobedience caused him to go on a detour, which led him into a destructive storm that caused unbelievers to offer devotion to God! Even in the midst of our disobedience, God can make a positive impact in the lives of those around us through the destruction that He allows to break out in our lives. You might be on the run from God, but He is able to take your rebellion and use it as an opportunity for someone to experience Him and even turn to Him for salvation.

A POWERFUL PARALLEL

The Holy Spirit revealed to me how this passage of Scripture in Jonah 1:4-16 parallels with Mark 4:35-41. When we compare these two passages of Scripture, we see that Jonah and Jesus were both on boats. Jonah was on his boat because of disobedience, Jesus was on his boat because of a destination— "Let's cross over to the other side of the sea" (Mark 4:35). Both of their boats contained other passengers. Jesus was with his disciples and Jonah was with the sailors. Jonah and Jesus took the same action and went to sleep on their boats. A storm arose on both occasions that threatened the structure of their vessels. For Jesus, it was a test of His disciples' faith. For Jonah, it was a trial that would turn the faith of the sailors to God. Both Jonah and Jesus were awakened out of their sleep by the men on their boats who were afraid of the storm.

Jonah was asked, "What are you doing sound asleep" (Jonah 1:6a)? Jesus was asked, "Teacher, don't you care that we are going to die" (Mark 4:38)? Jesus got up and spoke to His storm: "Silence! Be Still" (Mark 4:39)! Jonah had to surrender to his storm (Jonah 1:12,15). In the end, the sailors on Jonah's boat showed great fear unto the Lord (Jonah 1:16), as well as the disciples on Jesus' boat, provoking them to ask the question, "Who then is this? Even the wind and the sea obey Him" (Mark 4:41)!

There are times when it looks like our lives are parallel to the ways of Christ. When we take a closer look, we are operating under our own direction and making our own decisions, which results in us surrendering to the storm that compounds our lives due to our faithless journey apart from Christ. Proverbs 3:5-6 says, "Trust in the Lord with all your heart, and do not rely on your own understanding. In all your ways know Him, and He will make your paths straight."

Even in the moments when we are not comfortable about what God is calling us to do, the first thing we should do is seek Him for guidance and encouragement to accomplish His will (Matthew 6:33). God's plans and purposes for our lives are divinely orchestrated, even if it seems like it's too complicated to accomplish. The goal is to place our trust in Him, always, because He has all the answers, and He is our source for everything we need.

MAN OVERBOARD...INTO GOD'S WILL

Jonah 1:15- "Then they picked up Jonah and threw him into the sea, and the sea stopped its raging."

My three months of being a full-time babysitter had finally come to an end. Tonia and I took Christian home to New Jersey, and when we returned, I took a job as a life insurance agent. I felt I was on the right track of climbing out of the hole that I had dug myself into. My three months of watching Christian had taught me to be more responsible as well as patient. I was thankful for the new opportunity, and I was ready to get back to being a helpmate to my wife. I felt like the storm was finally going to settle. What I didn't realize was that my time with Christian not only fulfilled a purpose of being a guardian for him in his time of need, but it was also preparing me for what was about to come.

The insurance gig only lasted five months. I had sold a few policies, but it wasn't made thoroughly clear to me that I wouldn't receive any money until I reached a certain amount in commissions. I was very much displeased at this, and after four months, I finally got paid. Tonia and I decided that it would be best to let the position go and find something that paid a consistent salary. She was thankful for my effort to get back in the game and try to help out with the finances.

God was about to show up again, and in a very big way I didn't see coming. There was another baby I was about to encounter, and I wasn't ready for him because I was too focused on trying to get back on my feet. My time with Christian was also preparation for me to become a parent, not to a child of our own, but to Tonia's great nephew. Like Jonah, I was about to be thrown overboard into God's will. One thing I can say about being in God's will is that it isn't always pleasant, and sometimes you simply feel lost with no direction. The weight of the circumstances that were about to come would be devouring, but within the process, I would find a new love and gain a son. His name is Jeremiah, and his name means "The LORD will raise!"

CHAPTER 4

DESTRUCTION LEADS TO DEVOURING

"The LORD appointed a great fish to swallow Jonah, and Jonah was in the belly of the fish three days and three nights."

—Jonah 1:17

There are moments in life when your circumstances are so overwhelming, you simply don't have an answer, and you don't know what to do. There is nowhere to go and there seems to be no one around that can help with what you are facing. It's an uncomfortable place to be in, and at times, it can really feel as if you are being devoured. You are left appalled by being in such a place, but yet you are appointed to be there. When you find yourself in such a place, you are now in the will of God.

When I used to hear people talk about the will of God, I always assumed it was something good, prosperous, and fulfilling. All three are true about the will of God, but what I didn't know is that a journey would have to be taken to experience the fullness and goodness of His will. That journey takes you to unexpected places and puts you in uncertain positions. This is where God can do His best work because you are left solely to depend on Him and to use all that He provides for you. Be prepared whenever you pray for God's will to be done. Before the good comes out of it, you must first endure the gauntlet.

THE LORD WILL RAISE

On December 13, 2018, a new addition was added to the family. Our great nephew had entered into the world and his name was Jeremiah. We went down to the hospital the next night to visit, and I remember seeing this small new gift that God had given to the family! It was my turn to hold him, and as I held him in my arms, I silently prayed over him. I prayed that God would raise him in goodness and love and that God would protect him and provide for him. I prayed that God would bless him to grow up and become a follower of Jesus Christ and that he would be blessed with all he needed in order to succeed in life and to do well. To me, it was just a little simple prayer to pray over a newborn baby. You want the best for little babies, and you want their futures to be bright. As we left the hospital that night, I had no idea that God was about to place me in His will, and that this new bundle of joy would eventually become more than my great nephew.

Five months had passed, and I was in the midst of working for the insurance company. It wasn't going well, as I mentioned before, and I was struggling to find stability. One day while I was at the office, Tonia called and said she had something she needed to discuss with me once I got home. When I got home, she informed me she had received a call from our niece asking if we would get Jeremiah out of the foster care system. I was confused because I thought everything was going well with him and his mom. No one informed us he had been taken away from our niece.

I told Tonia I would pray about it. We had just taken Christian back home, and I wasn't interested in taking on someone else's child. I was too focused on trying to fix my issues and trying to get us back to a place of establishment. She followed up with me a day or so later, and I told her I was still praying about it. She was really being patient with me because I wasn't really interested in the situation, and it was a way to keep her at bay by saying I was praying about it.

She came to me again a few days later, but this time, she wanted a full conversation on the matter. We had a drag out dispute over the situation. I explained why I wasn't interested, and that it was nothing against Jeremiah. I simply felt we were in a bad place and needed to focus on us and our marriage. I didn't see how jumping into someone else's mess was going to help ours.

We went back and forth for a good hour on the issue. She finally hit me with the checkmate. Tonia is a very strong-willed woman, to the point she doesn't like to cry in front of me. She made the case that it would be unfair to Jeremiah to leave him in foster care, only for him to grow up and discover he had a family (a big family) in the area, and no one came to get him. As she was making her point, her emotions were pouring out and the tears were falling down her face like raindrops. She was determined to get her great nephew, whether I was on board or not.

I felt like a huge jerk after that. I wasn't trying to be one, I was just in a place of trying to "man up" and make things suitable for us again. This time, I actually prayed about it, and I told God that if this is what He wanted us to do, I would surrender to His will, and we would go and get Jeremiah. We informed our niece that we would get him out of foster care. She was elated and thanked us for stepping in.

We officially took temporary custody of Jeremiah in June of 2019. Our niece told us it would only be for three months. She had some legal obligations to take care of, and once she was done, she would be able to get him back. It seemed like something we could handle. Jeremiah was six months old at this point, and there was a lot of diaper changing and bottle feeding! Something was happening that I didn't see coming. I was heading into God's will, and it was about to surface in the form of a situation I had just departed from. I was about to become a full time babysitter once again, but this time, there would be greater responsibilities attached.

I eventually walked away from the insurance position. I wasn't making any money, and I wasn't gaining any clients. This created room for me to watch Jeremiah on a full-time basis. I felt a certain way about this because I was back in the same circumstance with a different baby. It was a bit more difficult, too, because he was an infant and needed constant attention, care, feeding, and being put down for naps throughout the day. It was exhausting, and I felt like God was punishing me.

Our niece had court-ordered, weekly visitations with Jeremiah. This required me to take him across town to the designated visiting site. It got to the point that I treasured the days I didn't have to leave the house with him because, on certain days, I would have to pick our niece up, just so she could make it to other court-ordered appointments she had to attend. I didn't understand what was going on in my life. I didn't know what to ask God for, and I didn't have an angle to make a move that was suitable for me. I was in a place where I was overwhelmed. I felt like I was simply being devoured by the circumstances. I didn't realize it at the time, but God had me right where He wanted me to be, in the middle of His will, and none of it felt good or seemed promising.

THE REVEAL OF GOD'S WILL

God has several names that speak to the characteristics of His power. The name Jehovah means "The self-revealing God." Whenever you find yourself in a situation that is beyond comprehension and difficult, when you seek God for understanding, He will reveal Himself and make clear the reasons for the circumstances you are facing. Jeremiah had been in our care for six months and nothing was changing or getting better when it came to his mom. I spent many nights and days praying for understanding of what was going on and why Tonia and I were having to deal with it. There seemed to be no answer from God, just the everyday struggle and frustration of the situation.

One day I was sitting alone in the peace and quiet and God showed up to reveal Himself and His will. God told me to let the wall down that I had built up and to embrace Jeremiah because he wasn't just my great-nephew, he was my son whom God had sent to me. I had built up a wall around my heart because I didn't want to get attached to him. When we had Christian for those three months, I got very attached to him. When we took him home to New Jersey, our hearts broke because we felt like we were abandoning our child whom we'd spent three whole months building a bond with. I didn't want to get attached to another child until we had our own.

God reminded me of the night in the hospital when I held Jeremiah, and I prayed over him. God was simply answering my prayer, and He decided to give us the job of being the vessels that would provide the care, comfort, and stability that Jeremiah would need. My heart was humbled at what God had made known to me. It was an emotional moment because my dad wasn't around to help raise me, and God was giving me the opportunity to be something to Jeremiah that I never had. I no longer prayed about the situation we were in. Instead, I started praying for correction and commitment in order to be the dad Jeremiah would need. I wanted to make sure I made a godly impact in his life. After such a powerful revelation from God, I let my wall down and let my heart attach to Jeremiah. He was no longer my great-nephew; He was now my son!

It has been a blessing to watch Jeremiah grow. Before he goes to bed at night, I read a little Bible story to him, and then we say our prayers. I thank God every day for my son, and I truly look forward to seeing what God has in store for him as he continues to grow. Psalm 127:3 says, "Sons are indeed a heritage from the LORD, offspring, a reward." Jeremiah is indeed a gift that God gave to us and I'm thankful God chose us as the vessels for his nurturing.

In Psalm 40:8, David proclaims, "I delight to do your will, my God, and your instruction is deep within me." When God made His will clear to me, I took delight in fulfilling the role of being Jeremiah's dad. I found confidence in God to be someone I had no experience in being. I trusted God that I could come to Him and get whatever I needed so I wouldn't fail at the task that was placed before me. Tonia and I were both raised in single parent homes, and God was blessing us to provide Jeremiah with the experience of being raised in a two-parent home.

What I couldn't see from the beginning was now being rolled out like a red carpet. The lesson God taught me from all of it was that what seems like a burden can turn out to be a blessing. When you start peeling back the layers, you get to see all of the fruitful things God has placed within the circumstance.

Jonah was told the will of God up front, but he took no delight in it. His lack of delight caused him to be disobedient, which led him on a detour. The detour soon turned into a situation of destruction, and Jonah found himself devoured by a big fish. There was nowhere for him to go; there was no one who came to his rescue. God had Jonah right where He wanted him, in the middle of His will, right in the belly of a fish. One thing is for certain: no matter what you do or say, God's will is going to come your way.

THE SIGN OF JONAH

Jonah is in a dark and lonely place. There is no one around to help him, and there is no one he can call on. This place he has found himself in stinks, literally, and there seems to be no way out of it. Jonah is in the belly of a great fish, and there is nothing he can do about it. The will of God is in full effect because God has appointed a great fish to swallow Jonah and has appointed the time for Jonah to be in this circumstance: three days and three nights (Jonah 1:17). Jonah now knows for certain there is no running from the will of God.

When we find ourselves in overwhelming circumstances, we act like it's the end of the world, and we complain and continuously cry out to God. No one has ever been in a situation like Jonah. Can you imagine being swallowed by a massive fish and having to sit in its belly for three days and three nights? Jonah is in a horrible circumstance! He is surrounded by everything this fish has eaten, the smell is possibly indescribable, he can't see anything, and he has no idea where this fish is going or if he will even make it out of this situation alive. The good news for Jonah is that this is God's will, and God is still with him, even in this dark and uncertain moment.

There will be times in our lives when God allows our circumstances to devour us. Sometimes He allows it in response to our disobedience, and other times He allows it for our development. No matter the reason, the end result should always be a stronger faith in God and the ability to trust Him in whatever He has called you to do or wherever He has called you to go. When you experience God carrying you through your circumstances, you realize He is your source, and you truly start walking by faith in order to fulfill your purpose. Jonah might have had some fear in going to Nineveh and probably felt like God was sending him on a death mission. Through this experience, God is taking Jonah's disobedience and using it to develop him in order to fulfill the calling that God appointed to him. In the next chapter, we will see that in spite of being in a foul situation, Jonah decides to place his faith in God.

Jonah's plight was referenced by Jesus to make a powerful statement to the scribes and Pharisees who were asking Him for a sign. Jesus responded by saying, *"An evil and adulterous generation demands a sign, but no sign will be given to it except the sign of the prophet, Jonah. For as Jonah was in the belly of the huge fish three days and three nights, so the Son of Man will be in the heart of the earth three days and three nights. The men of Nineveh will stand up at the judgment with this generation and condemn it, because they repented at Jonah's preaching; and look, something greater than Jonah is here"* (Matthew 12:39-41).

What is Jesus saying here? Jesus is telling the scribes and Pharisees that Jonah was in a dark, dank, and destitute situation that was defeating, which should have ended in death. Instead, God delivered him from the belly of the great fish. Jonah went forth and preached and there was a response. Jonah probably even looked and smelled like what he had been through, which means he was a living testimony! Jesus was letting the scribes and Pharisees know that He, too, would face a dark and defeating situation that would lead to His death, but after three days and three nights, God would deliver Him from the grave. The only difference is that the citizens of Nineveh responded to Jonah's message after his deliverance from the belly of the great fish. People would continue to deny Christ, after His resurrection, and even to this day; yet He is greater than Jonah.

I don't know who you are or what you are going through, but I want to encourage you to wait on the Lord. Things might seem dark right now, and your situation might even stink, but God will deliver you from the belly of your burden. One of my favorite verses in the Bible is 1 Peter 5:10. It says, "The God of all grace, who called you to His eternal glory in Christ, will Himself restore, establish, strengthen, and support you after you have suffered a little while." When we come out of our situation, when we find peace, when we have hope, when our faith is elevated, it will all be hand-delivered to us by God *Himself*!

Jonah is in the dark; it's dank, and death seems imminent. Most people would prepare themselves to perish because such a circumstance seems final. Jonah remembers who it is that he worships, and in this moment of detriment, Jonah offers up devotion to God.

CHAPTER 5

DEVOURING LEADS TO DEVOTION

"Jonah prayed to the LORD his God from the belly of the fish."

—Jonah 2:1

After a good three months of being unemployed, God finally answered and gave me a new job. I didn't realize it until later on, but God was preparing me for a second chance. He was going to give me the opportunity to wait on Him and to seek Him so I could experience what it is like when He gets me out of situations as opposed to my own efforts.

I had spent those three months applying to various positions and I wasn't getting any answers. Tonia offered to assist me in my search by sending my resume out to positions she felt would be a good fit for me. I was ready to tap into my foolish male pride again and tell her, "Thanks, but no thanks, I got this." The Holy Spirit told me not to deny her, but to let her help me.

She sent my resume out to a few companies. The next day, I got a phone call from a recruiter at a local financial institution. We had a quick phone interview and then scheduled my in-person interview for the following day. After going through the interview process and clearing my background check, I was offered the job. I was excited and thankful to God that He had given me a job where I was actually going to get paid and didn't have to worry about commissions. God had used my wife to help me gain employment again. It was also His way of showing me how important my wife is to me and our marriage. She had tolerated my bad decisions and was still supporting me. God had to open my eyes to help me realize how much of a help she is to me and how much she truly loves me.

As I started to settle into my new position, it didn't take long for things to start feeling uneasy. What started out as a nice welcoming place, soon turned into a hostile and uncomfortable environment. I found myself being singled out a lot, and if I made a mistake, I was questioned as if I were a child. At this point, I couldn't respond like I did before. I had my wife and Jeremiah depending on me. I couldn't fail again and quit. There were days when I wanted to express my feelings but because I was thinking of my family, I kept my mouth shut and let the anger reside within. It was a very unwelcoming place, and it started to weigh on me emotionally and spiritually.

On the morning of my 37th birthday, The Holy Spirit put it on my heart to open up the Bible and read Psalm 37. In it, I found what I was going to need to carry me through my journey in this new position. I devoted myself to prayer during this season of testing, and The Holy Spirit revealed five actions of faith for me to live by from Psalm 37. I discovered I needed to trust in Him (v3), take delight in Him (v4), commit my ways to Him (v5), be silent before Him (v7) and wait for Him (v34).

The weight and weariness of showing up to this place was unbearable. If it was not for God giving me the strength to pray and to trust in the actions He gave me, I would have failed again. By His grace and mercy, I was able to endure the hardship for a whole year. During that time, I was praying for God's deliverance out of the misery. There were even times where I had interviews for new positions, but they didn't turn into open doors.

My faith in God wouldn't quit. I trusted in Him to answer. I would get disappointed and discouraged when opportunities didn't blossom, and I had to continue to show up to an unsettling atmosphere, but yet, I was determined to see God show up on my behalf. After a year of sitting in the suffering, God showed up! He allowed me to experience what it looks like when we wait on Him, and let me tell you, the weight was worth the wait.

JONAH PRAYS

Jonah is in a quiet, lonely place. It's not a pleasant place to be either. He has found himself in the belly of a great fish. This is a pitiful place to be, but it is also a proper place to be. The best way for us to have prayer and to commune with God is when it is quiet, and we are alone. Jonah's circumstance is foul, literally, but in the midst of it, he gets humble, and he prays. In Jonah 2:2 he says, "I called to the LORD in my distress, and He answered me. I cried out for help from deep inside Sheol; You heard my voice." Jonah is letting us know that when we cry out to God with a heart of sincerity, God will hear us. He is able to deliver us out of the mess that we find ourselves in. Even if He doesn't respond immediately, wait on Him, and have faith that He is coming to your rescue.

Jonah starts to describe the scenario of being thrown overboard and what happened after that. He does not credit the sailors with throwing him overboard but realizes that it was all God's doing. Jonah describes the experience by saying, "You threw me into the depths, into the heart of the seas, and the current overcame me. All Your breakers and Your billows swept over me" (Jonah 2:3).

Can you imagine the fear that Jonah experienced in that moment? Jonah could have drowned and been lost in the depths of the sea. The thought of powerful waves washing over you with little to no chance to catch your breath is terrifying! In the midst of our disobedience, sometimes God has to throw us overboard and let us suffer a little as the waves of life wash over us. It doesn't matter how good of a swimmer you are, you will always need the Lifeguard, Jesus Christ, to come and rescue you. In the midst of his drowning dilemma, Jonah seeks God, even though he feels he has been shut out from God's presence: "But I said, "I have been banished from your sight, yet I will look once more toward Your holy temple" (Jonah 2:4).

When your relationship with God is fruitful and your faith in Him is firm, nothing can separate you from Him. In Romans 8:38-39, Paul says, "For I am persuaded that neither death nor life, nor angels nor rulers, nor things present nor things to come, nor powers, nor height nor depth, nor any other created thing will be able to separate us from the love of God that is in Christ Jesus our Lord." Jonah was in the midst of drowning, dying, and feeling distant from God, yet he still sought God no matter what the outcome was about to be. If you truly trust in God and know who He is, you will always seek Him no matter how bad the situation gets.

This act also shows the faith that Jonah had. His faith in God caused him to look for God to rescue him. He believed that God would save him from the watery grave he was about to encounter. Your faith in God is vital. How vital you ask? Hebrews 11:6 says, "Without faith, it is impossible to please God, since the one who draws near to Him must believe that He exists and that He rewards those who seek Him." If we want to please God, we must have faith in Him to provide, protect, and produce in every aspect of our lives. Jonah's faith in God didn't waiver, even though the facts were telling a different story (Jonah 2:5-6).

Jonah was in the belly of the great fish for three days and three nights. That's a long time to be in a dark, dingy place with no one around and no food to eat, except what the fish has in its belly. Yet through all of this, Jonah remembers God and realizes he is now in God's will. He says, "As my life was fading away, I remembered the LORD, and my prayer came to You, to Your holy temple" (Jonah 2:7).

Jonah remembered all the great things the LORD had done for him. He remembered His power, His blessings, His calling on Jonah's life. When Jonah remembered these things, he prayed unto the LORD. When we veer from the path that God has designed for us, we will eventually find ourselves feeling lost and alone, maybe even hopeless. But when we remember God loves us and all of the things He has done for us, it rushes us back to His presence, and it places us back in His will with a heart of commitment. Jonah ends his prayer with a powerful proclamation and a vow: "Those who cherish worthless idols abandon their faithful love, but as for me, I will sacrifice to You with a voice of thanksgiving. I will fulfill what I have vowed. Salvation belongs to the LORD" (Jonah 2:8-9).

Jonah was in God's will, and he was ready to do God's will. He was ready for his second chance to serve God, and to do so faithfully. Jonah renounced his will and rendered himself unto God. By doing so, God set him free from his prison.

Jonah 2:10 says, "Then the LORD commanded the fish, and it vomited Jonah onto dry land." There is no greater feeling than when God shows up to set you free from a circumstance that simply overwhelms you and seems like there is no way out. With our freedom, comes a response of faith to God. He is giving us the opportunity, or in some cases like Jonah, a second chance, to go forth and to live for Him and to fulfill the calling He has placed on our lives.

At the beginning of the chapter, I told you God finally showed up on my behalf. When He showed up, it was suddenly! I got home from work one evening, and I was checking my emails. I noticed I had an email from a recruiter at another local financial institution. I responded, and the whole process of interviewing and being offered the position was done within a week. I was brought onboard as a Level Two in the Corporate Trust Operations Department, and the pay was $4 more an hour than what I was making.

After being on the job for four months, I got a 10-cent raise, which isn't much, but I thanked God for it. In that same month,

I took over the area of handling all the new business issues that came in. After one year of employment, I received a 10% raise. A few months after that, I was recruited by the Wealth Division of Corporate Trust. I accepted the offer and gained a promotion. I waited for God to respond, and He did. And I know that He isn't finished yet! I thank God every day for His deliverance and my response is to go forth sharing the Gospel and living in a manner that is pleasing and glorifying to Him and His Kingdom that is to come.

Jonah has been delivered from the belly of the great fish, but there is still a message to be delivered, and he still has to preach this message to the Ninevites. After a failing flee and a pitiful plight, Jonah has regained his faith in the LORD and is now ready to step into his destination.

CHAPTER 6

DEVOTION LEADS TO DESTINATION

The word of the LORD came to Jonah a second time: "Get up! Go to the great city of Nineveh and preach the message that I tell you."

—Jonah 3:1

We serve a God who gives us repeat chances to right the wrongs we have made in our lives. There will be times on this journey of life when we fail, and we don't meet the expectations God has required of us. Because of His grace and mercy, He extends an invitation for us to try again and succeed.

God moved in a mighty way on my behalf, and I realized what He actually did for me. He had given me a second chance at experiencing His power. I ran off and tried things my way, and you read how that turned out for me. While sitting in the midst of my circumstance, God was giving me another chance to seek Him and to wait for Him. I had to trust in Him that He would get me out and that He would provide better opportunities.

My second chance proved to be fruitful, and it has been a blessing to see His faithfulness continue to pour out upon me because of my obedience. My second chance also taught me how important it is to wait on the Lord. When we go our own way and try to do things apart from Him, it never works out well, and in due time, we will be seeking Him to help us out of the mess we have gotten ourselves into. When we wait on the Lord, we are letting Him know that we trust in Him and His plans that He has established for us. Isaiah 40:31 says, "But those who trust in the LORD will renew their strength; they will soar on wings like eagles; they will run and not become weary, they will walk and not faint."

Did you notice the benefits that you receive from trusting in the Lord? The first thing it says is that your strength will be renewed. Waiting on the Lord is not an easy thing to do. At times, the waiting gets so intense, you become persuaded that He is not there or that He doesn't care what you are going through. This can cause you to grow weak in your faith, weak in your praying, and weak in your decision-making. God always shows up on time, and He renews your strength so that you remain strong in these areas of faith while you are waiting on Him to show up. It also says that you will soar on wings like eagles. Have you ever seen an eagle soar? It is a beautiful site to see! They stretch out their wings, and they soar high above the trees, and it looks so effortless and graceful. The strength of God will cause you to soar high above your problems, and He will make it look effortless and graceful. You will recognize that He is the one carrying you through the plight of your journey.

The verse also says you will run and not become weary. I like to go jogging outside. It feels good getting a nice stride going and breaking a good sweat. The further I go, I eventually get winded, and I have to stop and walk for a bit to regain my breath. After I catch my breath, I'm re-energized, and I am able to go again for a good distance. On our spiritual journey, the situations and circumstances of life can leave us winded. At times, we feel we need to stop or step away from it all because it just seems too much to bear. God will give us a second wind to keep our spiritual stride so that we don't become weary and eventually give up. He is the strength that keeps us pressing forward in the midst of uncertainty.

The final benefit from the passage of Scripture says you will walk and not faint. Walking is a good way to relieve stress or to go out and enjoy nature on a beautiful day. If you actually had a destination to get to and you were going to walk to get there, it would eventually become exhausting, especially if your destination is far away. Walking by faith is a long journey. The things we anticipate and believe God for seem to take forever. We get tired of waiting, and soon enough, we get tired of faith-walking. Something that I noticed on my journey was that my hope in God would not die. I had become so anchored into Him being my answer, that nothing was going to deter my hope, even though I was getting tired of waiting and walking by faith.

I didn't know it at the time, but me choosing to wait on Him extended the opportunity for God to renew my strength, soar above the problems and pain I was facing, run and not tire out and to keep walking faithfully, even though I didn't see the outcome. While I was waiting for Him, He was working on me. He was restoring my faith and trust in Him, and I haven't taken it for granted at all. God eventually changed my circumstances, but before He did that, He had to change me.

We always want God to change our situation, which is fine, but God knows that before the situation changes, we need to be changed. Why is that? Because God will not take you somewhere new with an old perspective. If God would have answered me the first time, I cried out to Him, I would have left the job being prideful and would have carried that same energy and mindset to the next place.

God had to let me sit in it for a while so that I would humble myself and realize that the deliverance had nothing to do with me, but that it was all on Him. My perspective changed, and I thank Him every day for my new position, and I show up every day with a humble attitude. I realize that I wouldn't be there without Him making a way. God might not change your situation right away, and if not, don't lose heart. Pay attention and stay close to Him because He is probably working on you before He works it all out in your favor.

JONAH PREACHES

I enjoy a good sermon. It is refreshing to hear the Word of God preached in Spirit and in truth. Preaching is not something you do for fun. Preaching is not something you do to make friends. Preaching is not something you do to get financial gain. Preaching is a calling from God to go forth and preach the Gospel of Jesus Christ. The secular world considers the preaching of the cross to be foolish, but God uses this so called "foolishness" as a means towards salvation. 1 Corinthians 1:20-21 says, "Where is the one who is wise? Where is the teacher of the law? Where is the debater of this age? Hasn't God made the world's wisdom foolish? For since, in God's wisdom, the world did not know God through wisdom, God was pleased to save those who believe through the foolishness of what is preached."

You should pray for your pastor who has to stand before the congregation each Sunday and preach the Gospel. What they are called to do is no small task, and it requires continuous preparation week after week. Not only that, they have to preach the Gospel even when they don't feel like it. 2 Timothy 4:2-5 gives us more insight into this. Verse two gives the pastor his petition (*preach the Word*), his persistency (*be ready in season and out of season*) and his purpose (*rebuke, correct, and encourage with great patience and teaching*). Verses three and four let the pastor know that he must preach like this because there is a problem with the people's preference (*For the time will come when people will not tolerate sound doctrine, but according to their own desires, will multiply teachers for themselves because they have an itch to hear what they want to hear. They will turn away from hearing the truth and will turn aside to myths*). Regardless of such things taking place, verse five encourages the pastor to persevere (*But as for you, exercise self-control in everything, endure hardship, do the work of an evangelist, fulfill your ministry*).

What a powerful calling and work preaching is! If God has not called you to do it, I strongly encourage you not to go on your own accord. If you are preaching and you know God didn't call you to do it, step away and seek God faithfully for what He has actually called you to do. James 3:1-2 says, "Not many should become teachers, my brothers, because you know that we will receive a stricter judgment. For we all stumble in many ways. If anyone does not stumble in what he says, he is mature, able also to control the whole body." When God calls people to preach or teach the Gospel, a stricter responsibility is placed upon them. What you say and how you live your life can be an influence on others, in a good way or bad way. If you are teaching, preaching, or living in a manner that causes others to stumble or go astray from the faith, God will hold you accountable for such an offense.

Jonah has been given a second chance by God to do what God called him to do the first time: Go to Nineveh and preach. This time, Jonah was obedient to the command and went to Nineveh. Can you imagine what Jonah looks like at this moment? He is fresh out of the belly of the great fish, he's dripping wet, he's covered in seaweed and fish guts, and he stinks. He must have been a sight to behold and to smell! He is walking through this great city, which takes three days to walk around (Jonah 3:3).

On his first day of walking around the city, Jonah preaches probably the shortest sermon in the history of sermons. Jonah 3:4 says, "Jonah set out on the first day of his walk in the city and proclaimed, "In forty days Nineveh will be demolished!" Within this short sermon is a two-part message. Jonah is letting the people of Nineveh know there is bad news and good news. The bad news is God is bringing persecution upon their land. The good news is they have 40 days to prepare or to repent.

I'm pretty sure Jonah had a deep hope that the people wouldn't respond, and that God's judgment would be poured out upon them. We carry those same sentiments towards people whom we deem as undeserving of God's love, grace, and mercy. God gives everyone a fair chance to come to Him and to repent. The people of Nineveh needed an opportunity to hear the message of God and to make a choice on how they were going to respond, and Jonah was the prophet that God chose for this moment of service.

Romans 10:14-15 says, "How, then, can they call on Him they have not believed in? And how can they believe without hearing about Him? And how can they hear without a preacher? And how can they preach unless they are sent? As it is written: How beautiful are the feet of those who bring good news." Jonah wasn't being picked on or disregarded when God called him to go and preach to his enemies. Jonah was anointed for this purpose, and God's Word doesn't discriminate. God was more concerned about the hearts of the people of Nineveh instead of their horrible behavior. If Jonah doesn't preach to the people, the opportunity to repent of their sins would be denied.

There are so many people walking around who are lost, spiritually, because no one has shared the Gospel with them. Sometimes our pride and prejudice get in the way of doing the plans and purposes of God. How many times has God placed you in a position to minister to someone, but because you didn't like their attitude or because they were homeless or looked unapproachable, you disregarded the opportunity? We have all done it at one time or another. It is in those moments that God is showing us that we need more spiritual growth and that we also have issues of the heart that need to be addressed. This was another reason why God called Jonah to go to Nineveh. Not only did God want him to preach to his enemies, God wanted to show Jonah he had a problem of the heart, unsuitable for ministry.

If we believe in the power of the Gospel, then we should share it with no shame. Romans 1:16 says, "For I am not ashamed of the Gospel, because it is the power of God for salvation to everyone who believes, first to the Jew, and also to the Greek." We should also live our lives in such a way that it represents the Gospel. Philippians 1:27a says, "Just one thing: As citizens of heaven, live your life worthy of the Gospel of Christ." When God is moving on your heart to share the Gospel, pray for His strength and His words to take over so that His will may be done. You could say something, or do something, that ends up being life changing for someone, which gives you an opportunity to testify to the goodness of God and how He used you in a mighty way.

NINEVEH RESPONDS

Jonah preached his short and straight to the point sermon to the people of Nineveh. What happened in return was something powerful that Jonah was able to bear witness to: the people responded and prepared themselves for repentance!

Jonah 3:5 says, "Then the people of Nineveh believed God. They proclaimed a fast and dressed in sackcloth ... from the greatest of them to the least." The whole city of Nineveh responded to Jonah's sermon. From the richest person to the poorest, everyone took heed to God's Word. Jonah's message reached the King of Nineveh and even he responded by taking off his royal robe and putting on sackcloth and sitting in ashes (Jonah 3:6).

The king went even further and sent out a decree among the people of Nineveh. The king's decree said: *By order of the king and his nobles: No person or animal, herd, or flock, is to taste anything at all. They must not eat or drink water. Furthermore, both people and animals must be covered with sackcloth, and everyone must call out earnestly to God. Each must turn from his evil ways and his wrongdoing. Who knows? God may turn and relent; He may turn from His burning anger so that we will not perish* (Jonah 3:7-9).

Romans 10:17 says, "So Faith comes from what is heard, and what is heard comes through the message about Christ." There is a difference between listening and hearing. When you hear something, it causes you to respond. When you are driving down the street, and you hear the sirens of an emergency vehicle, you respond by moving to the side of the road so it can pass by. When we hear the Word of God, it should cause us to respond and to do so faithfully. The people of Nineveh heard the Word of God preached by Jonah, and they responded. The king took God's Word so seriously that he didn't want the people, or animals, eating or drinking. He wanted everyone, and every animal, covered in sackcloth and crying out to God for forgiveness of their sins. The sight of Jonah and the message of destruction he delivered was enough to get the people's attention. His message was clear: God was serious, and they should respond by repenting.

The people of Nineveh responded in a faithful manner and repented for their sins. What was God's response? Jonah 3:10 says, "God saw their actions, that they had turned from their evil ways, so God relented from the disaster He had threatened them with. And He did not do it." It wasn't the actions of putting on sackcloth that caused God to relent. God saw the sincerity in their hearts to repent, which led them to take the actions of putting on sackcloth and sitting in ashes. When we repent, we are telling God He is right about the sins we are committing. And in turn, we redirect our lives and our behavior in a direction that represents Him and pleases Him so that His will for our lives can be made manifest.

No matter who you are, what you have done, or what you might be doing right now, God is calling all of us to a place of repentance. Each day is a God given opportunity to repent of our sins and to start living our lives for Jesus Christ. 2 Peter 3:9 tells us, "The Lord does not delay His promise, as some understand delay, but is patient with you, not wanting any to perish but all to come to repentance." This delay refers to God's judgment that will come. It is indeed coming, but God loves each of us so much, that He is delaying the coming of His judgment so that all have an opportunity to repent and receive salvation.

To give you a picture, imagine that Jesus is standing in an elevator that is going up, and He is holding the door open for everyone who wants to come. He sees you standing in the distance, but He is holding the door open for you to come. As kind as it is of Him to do so, He can't hold the door open forever. Eventually, the door must close, and it will be too late to catch the ride up.

During the summer of 1994, my sister, Krisna, and I went to visit our cousins in Saginaw, Michigan. One Saturday morning, we went out with some of the members of the church to go witnessing to the people in the neighborhood. We came to one lady's house, and the leaders of the group were talking to her about Jesus and receiving salvation. When they got done talking to her, the only response she gave was that it was too late for her. I was only 11 years old, and I didn't know much about the Bible, but I knew it wasn't too late. I spoke up and told her "No, it's not too late, you still have time!" She continuously insisted to us that it was too late for her, and that Jesus could not use her. I remember walking away, and it bothered me deep down inside that she had counted herself as lost without even giving Jesus a chance.

My friend, if you are reading this, and you have not repented of your sins and accepted Jesus Christ as your Lord and Savior, I encourage you to do so immediately! It is not too late, so please don't miss the elevator. God is holding the door open for you; all you have to do is come, and He will receive you as His own. You can say this simple prayer unto God to receive salvation: *"Lord Jesus, I am a sinner in need of Your saving grace. Forgive me of my sins, and I ask that You come into my life and renew my heart and my mind. I accept Your sacrifice on the cross as payment for my sins, and I ask for the free gift of salvation that only You can give me. In Jesus name I pray, Amen."* If you sincerely prayed this prayer, I welcome you into the family of Jesus Christ, and I pray that every moment going forward is filled with His power and presence permeating through your life!

JONAH GETS ANGRY

Jonah did what God called him to do. He preached the Word of God to the people of Nineveh, and in return, they responded by repenting. Hallelujah! A whole city repents of its sins and turns to God! This is a time for celebration and praise! Jesus said in Luke 15:10, "I tell you, in the same way, there is joy in the presence of God's angels over one sinner who repents." There must have been a grand celebration in heaven if a whole city repented. But everyone was not happy about this occasion. The man that spoke the message of repentance to the people is now angry about the outcome.

Jonah 4:1 says that "Jonah was greatly displeased and became furious." What a strange response towards people who have turned away from their sins and have now turned to God. True enough, the people of Nineveh were considered to be Jonah's enemies, but God has done something amazing. Jonah is so displeased, that he lets God know it's the main reason why he took off running in the first place. He prayed to the LORD: "Please, LORD, isn't this what I thought while I was still in my own country? That's why I fled toward Tarshish in the first place. I knew that You are a gracious and compassionate God, slow to anger, abounding in faithful love, and one who relents from sending disaster" (Jonah 4:2).

Jonah knew all of these things about God, yet he fled when the call came to go and preach to his enemies. In other words, Jonah knew that God was going to forgive them, but Jonah wanted no part of their repentance. He took his chances of running instead of responding faithfully to what God was calling him to do. Jonah was so angry about the whole ordeal that he said, "And now, LORD, take my life from me, for it is better for me to die than to live" (Jonah 4:3). Jonah's anger was so intense, he preferred death over watching his enemies get deliverance. There is more going on here than just Jonah and the people of Nineveh being enemies.

Jonah has a heart problem, and whenever we have a heart problem, God must do some deep digging within us to get to the problem of the heart.

ONE AND DONE

There is something amazing about this preaching opportunity that God had given to Jonah. Jonah preached one message, a short message, and a whole city responded. When you look at the other major and minor prophets throughout the Bible, they preached and prophesied for years and had no success in getting the people to respond. Jonah is the only prophet who succeeded in gaining a response, and God blessed him to do so after one sermon. Of course, Jonah didn't know this, but if he did, I'm pretty sure he would have found great reason to give God praise instead of a pout.

The LORD asked, "Is it right for you to be angry" (Jonah 4:4)? There are times in our lives when God does something we don't like, and we get angry with Him about it. It is in those moments that God is proposing the same question to us that He asked Jonah. Do we really have a right to be angry? The sovereignty of God can leave us feeling salty, at times, causing us to display an attitude of selfishness.

Ephesians 4:26-27 says, "Be angry and do not sin. Don't let the sun go down on your anger, and don't give the devil an opportunity." There are going to be things, and people who do things, which will make us angry. We are entitled to our anger because it is an emotion. When we feed into that anger and dwell on the circumstances of the situation, we are now sinning and presenting the devil with an opportunity to lead us into an act, or saying words, that could cause harm to someone. When God does something we don't like, or does something opposite of what we were expecting, we get mad at Him for the one time that He said "no" and forget all about the other times that He said "yes."

That one "no" causes us to be done with being faithful, done with praying, done with reading the Bible, done with letting our light shine bright for Him and His kingdom. We become petty in our pouting. These are the moments where God wants to address the problems of our hearts and to let us know our anger truly isn't as justified as we think it is.

So, what is the problem of Jonah's heart that has him so angry? Jonah was prejudice towards the Ninevites. Because he did not like the Ninevites, Jonah held a preconception about them. They were violent and evil people, and as far as he was concerned, nothing good should come to them. It was the prejudice of his heart that sent him on this journey, and now, God wants to deal with that issue.

Jonah didn't even bother to answer God's question. Jonah 4:5 says that "Jonah left the city and found a place east of it. He made himself a shelter there and sat in its shade to see what would happen to the city."

Jonah's prejudice has truly put his heart in a dark place. It's one thing to leave the city and head home, but he left the city and set up shop at a distance to watch and see if anything bad would happen to the people of Nineveh. He was hopeful that their act of repentance wouldn't last, and it would cause God to reign down destruction.

Jeremiah 17:9 lets us know that "The heart is more deceitful than anything else and incurable-who can understand it?" We are instructed in Proverbs 4:23 to "Guard your heart above all else, for it is the source of life." We must guard our hearts against any ill issues that can come in and cause us to display a poor representation of Christ.

When we look at our world today, there are issues of racism, prejudice, injustice, greed, etc. that continue to cripple our society. There are some who proclaim Christ but refuse to witness to other people because of their skin color or because they are someone who is not well off and lives in poverty. We even have false religions that spread a theology that God only favors people who have a specific skin color and everyone else doesn't count. Such beliefs and practices stem from a lack of studying what God's Word truly says as well as people's hearts being polluted with issues that need to be addressed.

GOD'S PERSPECTIVE

For those of us who say that we are Christians, there should be no room within our hearts for biased behavior towards others. We serve a God who is not partial when it comes to humanity (Romans 2:11). If God shows no favoritism, then neither should we. There are times when we find ourselves being like Jonah. Jonah wasn't praying for the people of Nineveh to stay in favor with God. Instead, he was "*preying*" on them and hoping for their downfall. We might not necessarily go and pitch a tent and watch people from a distance, but when we refuse to minister to people because of biased issues residing in our hearts, we are "preying" on them and bypassing an opportunity for them to be redeemed.

God loves every one of us and the proof of that is in His Son, Jesus, dying on the cross for our sins (John 3:16). Jesus didn't die on the cross exclusively for one particular race. Christ died for us all! The key phrase in John 3:16 is "...everyone who believes in Him will not perish but have eternal life." Christ died for us all because "...all have sinned and fall short of the glory of God" (Romans 3:23). If you really want to see how separated we are from God in our sins, just take a look at Romans 3:10-12. It says, "There is no one righteous, not even one. There is no one who understands; there is no one who seeks God. All have turned away; all alike have become worthless. There is no one who does what is good, not even one."

If you think you do good and have a good deal of righteousness, Isaiah 64:6 cancels that: "All of us have become like something unclean, and all our righteous acts are like a polluted garment; all of us wither like a leaf, and our iniquities carry us away like the wind." Jesus knew all of this when it came to all of us, and yet, was not deterred in displaying His love for us. Romans 5:8 says, "But God proves His own love for us in that while we were still sinners, Christ died for us." Thank You Jesus! He didn't have to do it, and He would have been well within His right not to, but I thank Him every day that He did.

So, what does it take to effectively minister the Gospel to everyone? It takes God's perspective. There are growing theologies that are teaching God is partial towards certain races, leaving everyone else doomed for hell. These are false theologies. Think about it: If God created nations of people, placed an eternal promise of salvation, for everyone, through Jesus Christ in His Word, but yet knows that such a salvation is exclusively set aside for a particular race, it would make God the cruelest being ever. It would mean that He lied to us in His Word, that

Jesus dying on the cross for all of humanity was a scam and the Holy Spirit is biased in whom He chooses to dwell.

To believe such things about God is a wrong way of thinking and believing in Him. God makes it clear in Isaiah 55:8 when He says, "For My thoughts are not your thoughts, and your ways are not My ways." When it comes to His Word, He says, "so My word that comes from My mouth will not return to Me empty, but it will accomplish what I please and will prosper in what I send it to do" (Isaiah 55:11).

The Word of God is the truth, the whole truth, and nothing but the truth. The whole Bible is inspired, or breathed out, by God (2 Timothy 3:16), so if you believe He is who He says He is, then you can trust His Word to be filled with absolute truth.

If we are going to have God's perspective when it comes to sharing the Gospel, we must realize that God doesn't care about the skin, He cares about what's within. In 1 Samuel 16, Samuel is on his way to Jesse's house to anoint one of his sons as the next king of Israel. When Samuel sees Jesse's oldest son, Eliab, he is for certain this is God's chosen man as the new king. In verse seven, God lets Samuel know that Eliab is not who He has chosen, and He lets Samuel know why: But the LORD said to Samuel, "Do not look at his appearance or his stature because I have rejected him. Humans do not see what the LORD sees, for humans see what is visible, but the LORD sees the heart."

Samuel was impressed with the outside, but God was looking on the inside. If we truly have a love for people, then we shouldn't care about their skin color, height, eye color, or hair color. We should be concerned with the inside, the salvation of their souls. Peter also spoke about this in Acts 15:8-9 when he said, "And God, who knows the heart, bore witness to them by giving them the Holy Spirit, just as He also did to us. He made no distinction between us and them, cleansing their hearts by faith." God does not care about our skin color; He cares about the condition of our hearts. Our skin color represents one of the countless, beautiful attributes of God's creativity!

If skin color mattered, then Jesus would have never ministered to the Samaritan woman at the well (John 4:1-42). The woman speaks to the issue in verse nine when she asks Jesus, "How is it that you, a Jew, ask for a drink from me, a Samaritan woman? For Jews do not associate with Samaritans." If skin color mattered, Philip, being led by the Holy Spirit, would have never gone to the Ethiopian to witness about Jesus Christ (Acts 8:26-39).

God is concerned with our hearts, and in order for hearts and minds to be changed, we must share the Gospel of Jesus Christ. If you are struggling with a bias towards certain people, hopefully this illustration will help address your issue: Let's say you are in a house that is engulfed with flames. There is heavy smoke and heat all around you, and there seems to be no way out. All of a sudden, you see someone coming in to help you. They eventually get you out and your life is spared, but they end up perishing.

Would it matter to you what the person looked like? Absolutely not! All you would care about is how they risked their life to save yours. You would be focused on the condition of their heart, which would be caring and compassionate, and not their skin color. Christ rushed in to save us all from a burning hell! When we get to heaven, we are not going to care about His skin color. We will be too busy loving on Him and thanking Him for all He did for us. Until that day, we should go forth sharing the good news with everyone of how wonderful Jesus is, because there are plenty of people that still need to be rescued from the unfortunate future of being eternally separated from God.

In Mark 13:10, Jesus says, "And it is necessary for the Gospel to be preached to all nations." The reason for this is because there is something beautiful when you read Revelation 5:9 and 7:9. Revelation 5:9 says, "And they sang a new song: You are worthy to take the scroll and to open its seals, because You were slaughtered, and You purchased people for God by Your blood from every tribe and language and people and nation." Revelation 7:9 says, "After this I looked, and there was a vast multitude from every nation, tribe, people, and language, which no one could number, standing before the throne and before the Lamb. They were clothed in white robes with palm branches in their hands." Did you catch that?

There will be a representative from every tribe, language, people, and nation in Heaven! How will this happen? Through the sharing of the Gospel.

You sharing the Gospel with a co-worker or neighbor could lead that person to finding their purpose in missionary work and ministering the Gospel to thousands of people in other countries. Maybe God blesses this book to go international and it changes lives in the far corners of the world. Whatever it is, God can take the little and do much with it if we are faithful in our efforts.

If you are struggling with a bias of racism, prejudice, partiality, or any other issue that keeps you from sharing the

Gospel, I strongly encourage you to repent of such issues resting within you and ask God to renew your heart, mind, and spirit for the sake of His Kingdom and for proper service in ministry. David prayed to God in Psalm 51:10, "God, create a clean heart for me and renew a steadfast spirit within me." I pray that you feel the power of God covering you and guiding you to share the Gospel and to be a light for Him like you never have before. No longer concerning yourself with the outside, but having a Christ-like compassion for the inside. God bless you my friend as you press forward in your good works for the Kingdom of God!

GOD'S PLANT LEADS TO GOD'S POINT

Jonah is angry. In this state of anger, Jonah is "preying" on his enemies instead of praying for them. God wants to deal with Jonah's issue, so He does something miraculous. Jonah 4:6a says, "Then the LORD God appointed a plant, and it grew over Jonah to provide shade for his head to rescue him from his trouble." In the midst of Jonah's heart condition, God provides comfort to calm him down. Jonah even takes great pleasure in the plant (Jonah 4:6b). The pleasure Jonah is experiencing from the plant won't last long, because eventually, God is going to make a point with this plant. "When dawn came the next day, God appointed a worm that attacked the plant, and it withered" (Jonah 4:7).

You might be siding with Jonah right now and thinking this is a cruel move by God. Jonah has spent three days in the belly of a great fish, he had to preach to his enemies, only to see them repent, and God finally gives him something to smile about and find comfort in, and the next day, God appoints a worm to destroy it. It seems like Jonah can't catch a break. God knows that Jonah needs more than a break. Jonah needs to be broken in order to deal with the issues of his heart. In order for that to happen, God must remind Jonah of who He is.

There will be times in our lives when God must remind us of who He is. We feel we are entitled to the things, people, and positions that we have while forgetting we only have such things because of God. Notice that Jonah was pleased with the plant, but it doesn't say Jonah told God thank you for the plant. Could Jonah have felt he deserved the plant after all he had been through?

It's a possibility. When life has been tough on us, and something good finally happens, it's easy for us to take the mindset that we deserve it. We don't recognize that the good thing has come from God, and we might forget to say, "Thank You."

James 1:17 says, "Every good and perfect gift is from above, coming down from the Father of Lights, who does not change like shifting shadows." We should always give thanks to God for what we have, and even for what we don't have, because He knows what is best for us. Even when you are going through trials and tribulations, give thanks to God for being with you and ask Him what it is He wants you to learn while you are going through your circumstance.

God is in the midst of reminding Jonah of who He is. When we look at Jonah 4:6, it says "the LORD God." Whenever we read the Bible and see "LORD" with all capital letters, it represents the Hebrew word "Jehovah," which means "The self-existing One." Whenever we see "God," it represents the Hebrew word "Elohim," which means "the strong Creator." When we put both words together, it says "The self-existing One who is the strong Creator." What a powerful name! God is self-existent, meaning He has always existed, and He has no origin. He is the strong creator because everything that exists is only able to exist because He created it. God alone is creator, and God alone is Sovereign.

Not only does God destroy the plant, but He also literally turns up the heat on Jonah!

Jonah 4:8 says, "As the sun was rising, God appointed a scorching east wind. The sun beat down on Jonah's head so much that he almost fainted, and he wanted to die. He said, "It's better for me to die than to live."

Jonah is overwhelmed with anger about the people of Nineveh and the plant. His anger has gotten so intense, he doesn't even ask God for mercy or relief when the sun starts beating down on him. He has found justification within himself to die in his anger. Not only does Jonah have an issue of prejudice, but he also has an issue of pride dwelling in his heart as well. Proverbs 16:18 says, "Pride comes before destruction, and an arrogant spirit before a fall." Jonah felt he was in the right about his anger. He felt it was right to be angry about everything that had happened.

I like to define pride as "self-justification." Self-justification is an effort to defend your actions or attitude, even when you know that you are in the wrong. You refuse to admit your mistake and you will defend your position to the end.

Some people even deflect from the issue in order to avoid being held responsible. This only works within humanity because there is no escaping God when it comes to being held responsible.

Romans 8:33 says, "Who can bring an accusation against God's elect? God is the one who justifies." If we are seeking to justify our own selves, we are out of place and full of pride. Only God can justify us. In the book of Job, Elihu got angry at Job over his self-justification. Job 32:2 says, "Then Elihu, son of Barachel the Buzite from the family of Ram, became angry. He was angry at Job because he had justified himself rather than God."

Then God asked Jonah, "Is it right for you to be angry about the plant?" This time, Jonah answers and says "Yes, it's right! I'm angry enough to die" (Jonah 4:9)! Jonah has once again missed the point because he is simply focused on himself and how he feels. He doesn't care about the people of Nineveh, and he doesn't care how God feels. All that matters in this moment is Jonah and his self-righteous anger. Since Jonah keeps missing the point, God is going to make the point clear to Jonah.

Jonah 4:10 says, "So the LORD said, "You cared about the plant, which you did not labor over and did not grow. It appeared in a night and perished in a night." God is reminding Jonah of who He is. He is the strong Creator. He appointed the plant to grow over Jonah, and He appointed the worm to come and destroy it the next day. Jonah had no input on the plant's existence. He simply got to enjoy the benefit of it at no cost or effort to him. This really speaks to how much we really need God. His blessings and benefits are so amazing, we can forget that none of it belongs to us. We are just blessed to experience the benefits of it at no cost.

Psalm 24:1 makes it clear by saying, "The earth and everything in it, the world and its inhabitants belong to the LORD."

God proposes a final question to Jonah: "But may I not care about the great city of Nineveh, which has more than a hundred and twenty thousand people who cannot distinguish between their right and their left, as well as many animals" (Jonah 4:11)? There is no answer recorded from Jonah. We don't know what happened to Jonah after this. Maybe he went back home or maybe he actually sat there and died in his anger. Nevertheless, God was making the point to Jonah that as the strong Creator, He has a right to care about His creation. Throughout this journey, God has been showing Jonah who He is. It was God who commanded Jonah to go preach, but when Jonah decided to rebel, it was God who appointed the storm, it was God who appointed the great fish, it was God who appointed the plant, it was God who appointed the worm, and it was God who appointed the scorching wind. God is in command of His creation, but He also cares for it.

God is letting Jonah know He has every right to care for the people of Nineveh because they are human beings living in sin who are in need of repentance. Jonah's heart was out of place when it came to the people of Nineveh. God even lets Jonah know there are more than 120,000 people, possibly little children and those with mental disabilities, who don't even know their right hand from their left, as well as many animals, and yet Jonah wanted to see all of them perish.

Is God trying to make a point in your life today? Are you struggling with the issues of your heart or with how God is operating in your life and circumstances? One thing we must remember is God loves us all. It doesn't matter how we might feel about someone, God loves them, and He wants to extend grace and salvation unto them. Make yourself available so God can use you, so your heart rejoices at His work instead of rejecting and rebelling against it.

If you are truly struggling with the issues of your heart, I encourage you to pray to God for help and also to read what His Word says about the heart. It is hard to be a true blessing unto others if bitterness resides within you. Stay strong in the faith my friend and take all of your issues to the Lord with sincerity. He is able to heal you and give you the understanding you need to prosper forth faithfully in life and in ministry.

CHAPTER 7

DOES YOUR DESTINATION LEAVE YOU DISAPPOINTED?

It was the summer of 2010. Tonia and I had been dating for over a year, and we were preparing to attend her family reunion. We took a seven-hour bus ride to Biloxi, Mississippi, and midway through the trip, the air went out on the bus, and we had to open up the windows. Everybody was sweating from the heat, which at times became unbearable. We finally arrived in Biloxi, and everyone was excited. As the bus got off at the exit, we saw the casinos, hotels, and restaurants. Everyone was ready for a good weekend of family, fun, food, and fellowship.

All of a sudden, the bus driver turns up one street and down another. He gets back on the main highway and starts going in the opposite direction. Ten minutes later, we pull into an abandoned parking lot. On the right side of the parking lot was a hotel. It was our hotel. When we all walked inside, disappointment set in.

The lobby was small, and it took the front desk workers forever to get us all checked in. We had reached our destination, but the outcome was not what we anticipated. Let's just say it set the tone for how the rest of the weekend would play out.

There is nothing like having an anticipation for something, only for it to end in disappointment. People date and form relationships with the anticipation of a happy marriage, but sometimes it turns out to be disappointing. Students study for hours on end with the confidence they will do well on their exam, but the grade they receive is disappointing. Parents raise their children with great love, adoration, and discipline, with the hope that they will become model citizens, but sometimes they turn out to be a disappointment.

God has called people into the ministry, to preach His Word, to serve others, to be a light bearer for the kingdom. They say "yes" to the call with an anticipation that everything will go their way, but the more they go along the journey, their destination leaves them disappointed.

Have you reached your destination? Are you disappointed? Have you asked God why He chose you to do what He called you to do? There are times when it seems like God has set us up to fail, but in reality, He's giving us a chance to function in our faith. We don't experience this because we are so focused on what we see, or don't see, and we forget to ask God to intervene and provide us with what we need in order to fulfill what we are called to do.

In John Chapter 6, Jesus had a crowd of 5,000 people who were hungry and needed to be fed. It looked like a disappointing situation because Philip said, "Two hundred denarii worth of bread wouldn't be enough for each of them to have a little" (verse 7). Peter's brother, Andrew, said, "There's a boy here who has five barley loaves and two fish—but what are they for so many" (verse 8)? The disciples saw a failing situation, but Jesus saw an opportunity to function in His faith. Jesus said, "Have the people sit down" (verse 10a).

Jesus was going to place His faith in the Father to fix the situation. I'm sure the disciples, as well the people, were concerned as to how this was going to work out for everybody. Jesus placed His faith in the Father when He gave the command for the people to sit down. The result was miraculous: *"Then Jesus took the loaves, and after giving thanks He distributed them to those who were seated-so also with the fish, as much as they wanted. When they were full, He told His disciples, "Collect the leftovers so that nothing is wasted." So, they collected them and filled twelve baskets with the pieces from the five barley loaves that were left over by those who had eaten" (John 6:11-13).*

When you are in the midst of an uncertain situation, your faith in God will cause Him to show up and magnify the situation. We have to learn how to get out of our feelings and move into an act of faith so that we can experience God beyond measure. When we stay in our feelings regarding the circumstances, we feel as if God is not with us, and it leaves us feeling disappointed.

After a few years of teaching Sunday School, class attendance started to dwindle. Week after week, I was studying the lesson and getting excited to share what God had given me to teach. When Sunday would come, there would only be myself, Tonia, and sometimes one or two other people in attendance. As time went on, I got more and more frustrated about it. I became so disappointed in it, that I eventually gave up teaching the class.

In hindsight, it was an opportunity for me to place my faith in God to intervene in the situation. Instead of praying and trusting that God would fill up the seats, I grew weary and walked away. God had destined me to teach Sunday School, but I was disappointed and felt like God had set me up. Let me share with you three things God has taught me over the past few years when it comes to reaching your destination, even if it leaves you disappointed.

1. CHOOSE FAITH OVER FEELINGS

Feelings. We all have them. Some days you feel happy and other days you feel sad. There are moments when you feel angry and uncertain about things and there are times when you feel content. Feelings are real. We can't tell someone they don't feel a certain way because we aren't in their bodies, and we don't know what's actually causing them to feel the way they are feeling. We must respect how people feel and find a proper way to address those feelings so both parties walk away with a mutual understanding.

What about faith and feelings? Can the two exist together? The answer is yes, but one deals with how you feel and the other deals with how you function. Depending on which one you choose to use, you can either please God or disappoint Him. You remember our friend Jonah? Jonah's feelings about the people of Nineveh were real. He didn't like them, and he didn't want anything to do with them. God was calling him to function in his faith when it came to ministering to the people of Nineveh. Instead, Jonah tapped into his feelings and decided to flee in the opposite direction.

I will be honest in telling you there will be times when God is calling you to function by faith, but your feelings will take precedence. There were times when I didn't feel like studying and preparing the Sunday School lesson. I felt like it was a waste of time due to the lack of people showing up. Instead of tapping into my feelings, I responded faithfully, and I got to experience God ministering His Word to me as I prepared the lesson.

Your faith should always override your feelings. God knows we are human, and we have our emotions. He understands we don't always feel like doing what needs to be done. When we choose to respond by faith, He gives us the strength and encouragement to accomplish what He is calling us to do.

When the time was approaching for Jesus to be crucified, He made His feelings clear when He said, "Father, if You are willing, take this cup away from Me." Jesus didn't feel like drinking from the cup because it was full of God's wrath. Jesus didn't want to feel the pain and persecution that was about to come His way. In that same moment, Jesus responded by faith and said, "nevertheless, not My will, but Yours, be done" (Luke 22:42). Once He decided to function in His faith and not His feelings, we see that "Then an angel from heaven appeared to Him, strengthening Him" (Luke 22:43).

We should give thanks to Jesus every day that He didn't settle for His feelings but was determined to function in His faith to please the Father. If Jesus would have settled for how He felt, we would all be doomed to Hell! Jesus knew the whole of humanity was at stake, and it was not a time to tap into His feelings. Doing the will of the Father is what mattered the most.

Maybe God has called you to a place and a purpose, but you're not feeling good about the opportunity. Maybe you feel it's too small, too far away, or maybe you even feel like it's going to be boring. God understands, but what He wants you to do is respond by faith. You can go to Him in prayer and let Him know how you are feeling about the situation, but in turn, ask Him to strengthen you to function by your faith and not according to your feelings. When you entrust yourself into the will and the way of God, you will experience His divine, wonder-working power in a way that leaves you testifying of His goodness!

2. WALK BY THE SPIRIT

One Sunday morning, I was on my way to Sunday School. As I was driving, I start feeling something drawing me to pull into the gas station I was approaching. I was confused because I didn't need gas, and I wasn't in the mood for any snacks. The draw was strong, and to my surprise, I found myself pulling into the gas station. I had no idea what was going on, and I was wondering why I had pulled into this gas station.

In the midst of wondering what was happening, a Hispanic woman was waving and trying to get my attention. As I got out of the vehicle, I see that the front bumper on her vehicle has partially come off, which was preventing her from driving forward. She didn't really speak English, but she motioned with her hands asking if I could tear the bumper off. I nodded my head yes, removed the bumper, and she smiled at me and said "Gracias!" As I got back in the car to head to church, I realized the strong draw I had felt was the Holy Spirit guiding me to a place I wasn't interested in going because someone was there who was in need of help.

There are going to be times on your spiritual journey when the Holy Spirit is going to send you somewhere you don't want to go or will send someone your way you are not in the mood to deal with. When these moments come, you have two options: walk by the Spirit or walk in the flesh. The easy option is to walk in the flesh, especially if you are in a bad mood or you have plans you want to make sure get accomplished. The best thing to do is to walk by the Spirit. Doing so allows God to show up in the circumstance and to lead your words, thoughts, actions, attitude, and motives.

Galatians 5:16-17 says, "I say then, walk by the Spirit and you will certainly not carry out the desire of the flesh. For the flesh desires what is against the Spirit, and the Spirit desires what is against the flesh; these are opposed to each other, so that you don't do what you want." Walking by the Spirit isn't just something you should consider. If you are a born-again believer in Jesus Christ, walking by the Spirit should be a way of life for you. It keeps you at peace when facing difficult decisions, and it leads your heart to trust in Jesus when you don't see or understand how things are going to work out. It's the Holy Spirit responding instead of you responding to the matter.

When we walk by the Spirit, we become living witnesses to the fruit He is bearing within our lives. Galatians 5:22-23 says, "But the fruit of the Spirit is love, joy, peace, patience, kindness, goodness, faithfulness, gentleness, and self- control. The law is not against such things." All of these elements are one fruit that help us to stay humble and to be holy (Leviticus 11:44). How do you know when you are walking by Spirit? When you encounter a situation, or a person, who would normally cause you to respond with anger or hostility, but instead, you respond with a calmness, or you don't respond at all. Your natural reaction is still within you, but because you are walking by the Spirit, you have given Him full permission to speak and react on your behalf.

It is not always easy to walk by the Spirit, especially since the flesh is still active and stands in opposition to the Spirit. If we choose to walk in the flesh, we may gain a moment of satisfaction from what we have said or done, but it closes the door on the Holy Spirit and His guidance and leaves us to our own destructive decisions.

To walk in the flesh is to walk in your own counsel, which is never good. We think we know what we are doing, but the only thing we are truly doing is creating chaos in our lives as well as in the lives of others. We should seek to walk by the Spirit because He is "a Spirit of wisdom and understanding, a Spirit of counsel and strength, a Spirit of knowledge, and of the fear of the LORD" (Isaiah 11:2).

We can depend on the Holy Spirit for everything we need on our spiritual journey towards our destination and to be the comfort and strength we need to fulfill our calling. Jesus lets us know that, as believers, we have someone special who leads us and guides us each day. Jesus said, "He is the Spirit of truth. The world is unable to receive Him because it doesn't see Him or know Him. But you do know Him, because He remains with you and will be in you" (John 14:17).

3. TRUST JESUS...NO MATTER WHAT

In Luke Chapter 23:39-43, there is an interesting dialogue that takes place. Jesus has been hung up on the cross in between two thieves. These two thieves shared a life of crime together, but they hold different perspectives when it comes to who Jesus really is. The first thief asks Jesus, "Aren't You the Messiah?" He then tells Jesus to "save Yourself and us" (verse 39)! The second thief rebukes his friend and says, "Don't you even fear God, since you are undergoing the same punishment? We are punished justly, because we're getting back what we deserve for the things we did, but this man has done nothing wrong" (verses 40-41). The second thief then says "Jesus, remember me when You come into Your kingdom" (verse 42)! Jesus, in return, gives the second thief a powerful promise by saying "Truly I tell you, today you will be with Me in paradise" (verse 43).

When we take a closer look, we can see the first thief held his doubts about who Jesus was. If we look at his perspective, he sort of has a point. The celebrity of Jesus had filled the area so I'm pretty sure he heard about Jesus turning water into wine, healing the sick, casting out demons, feeding 5,000 people, raising the dead, etc. None of those things seem to matter now because this great man, whom everyone has been following around and listening to, is in the same situation as he is, and it doesn't seem like Jesus can overcome the odds. This causes the thief to question Jesus and to doubt the claims He made about Himself.

The second thief carries a different perspective. In the midst of a literal dead situation, he chooses to trust that Jesus is who He says He is. While the first thief doesn't believe Jesus can help him, especially if He isn't able to help Himself, the second thief chooses to believe Jesus can deliver him. The one thing the thieves had in common is that Jesus was in the midst of the situation with them, but their individual perspectives about Jesus set them apart, faithfully, and eternally.

As you are on your faith journey towards your destiny, there will be days when you will feel like the first thief. You know that Jesus is in the midst of the circumstance with you, but it feels like He isn't doing anything or saying anything, no matter how much you pray and cry out. These are tough moments to experience, but if you don't anchor down in your faith, you could easily develop the perspective of the first thief and start to doubt that Jesus can and will do anything for you. Continue to wait on Jesus and know He is working things out on your behalf, even when you can't see it.

We should strive to have the faith and perspective of the second thief. We should understand Jesus is in the midst of the circumstance, and even if it seems like a losing situation, we should trust Him to deliver us out.

The first passage of Scripture showed that we can either doubt Jesus or depend on Him, depending on our perspective. In this second passage of Scripture, we will see that we can show faith towards Christ, but depending on our plight, our faith can be firm or feeble.

Life will deal us various trials, and at times, our situation can seem like something that just will not settle. Our plight becomes problematic, and even though we are seeking Jesus in our prayers, our faith might not be as fully invested in Him as it should be.

We are all familiar with the story of the woman with the issue of blood in Mark Chapter 5. The sermons I have heard preached about her have all been good, but what I didn't realize was there was a situation already in progress before she showed up. There was a synagogue leader, named Jairus, who came to Jesus because his daughter was sick and dying. He pleads for Jesus to come to his house to heal her, which Jesus agrees to do (Mark 5:21-24). The woman with the issue of blood suddenly shows up and disrupts the journey to Jairus' house.

The woman with the issue of blood might seem like a problem for Jairus, given his plight, but what takes place will turn out to be what he needs in order to truly have faith in Jesus. This woman has endured her situation for twelve years, spent all her money on the doctors, but got no help, and eventually her situation turned worse (Mark 5:25-26). Regardless of everything she had been through, she heard about Jesus and made a firm move of faith. The woman said, "If I just touch His clothes, I'll be made well" (Mark 5:28). The woman was instantly healed of her affliction! She didn't say she needed to touch Jesus or to even see Him. She had so much faith in Him being able to heal her, all she needed was to touch His clothes. She doesn't get to walk away unnoticed though. She took the leap of faith to touch Jesus's clothes, and now it's her time to testify.

Mark 5:30 says, "At once Jesus realized in Himself that power had gone out from Him. He turned around in the crowd and said, "Who touched My clothes?" The disciples were baffled at the question because there were so many people around. They said, "You see the crowd pressing against You, and yet You say, 'Who touched Me'" (Mark 5:31)?

Jesus isn't asking the question because He doesn't know. He's God, which means He's omniscient, which means He knows everything. What He is doing is inviting the woman to reveal herself to the crowd and testify about her plight and how it suddenly changed through an act of faith in Him. Mark 5:33 says, "The woman, with fear and trembling, knowing what had happened to her, came and fell down before Him, and told Him the whole truth." Jesus responds by saying, "Daughter, your faith has saved you. Go in peace and be healed from your affliction" (Mark 5:34).

Notice Jesus tells the woman her faith saved her. Having firm faith in Jesus, in spite of your plight, is indeed a lifesaver. Jesus talks about having faith in God and the power that comes from it. He says in Mark 11:22-24, "Have faith in God. Truly I tell you, if anyone says to this mountain, 'Be lifted up and thrown into the sea,' and does not doubt in his heart, but believes that what he says will happen, it will be done for him. Therefore, I tell you, everything you pray and ask for—believe that you have received it, and it will be yours."

The mountains we face can be various things such as our jobs, people, finances, health, etc. Whatever your mountain is, you can remove it from your life through faith in Jesus Christ. The woman with the issue of blood had so much faith in Jesus, she was able to see her twelve-year mountain be removed immediately. Faith in Christ will take you places, and open up doors, but you must believe in Him with your whole heart in order to experience the mighty and miraculous.

Let's not forget about Jairus. Can you imagine how he is feeling right now? He has come to Jesus to help his sick and dying daughter, and along the way, this woman catches everyone's attention by touching Jesus's clothes. Not only is she testifying about her whole life, but time is also running out for his daughter. What looks like a fitting moment for Jairus to panic is actually a moment for him to pay attention and to praise the Lord. What the woman is saying should be giving him hope for his own plight, but sometimes the facts of the matter are too much, and our faith can easily turn feeble.

Jairus is still standing with Jesus, waiting for his turn to experience a miracle. While he is waiting, people from his house start walking up. Mark 5:35 says, "While He was still speaking, people came from the synagogue leader's house and said, "Your daughter is dead. Why bother the teacher anymore?"

Sometimes when you are walking by faith, family and friends can come along with the daunting facts of the circumstance, and if you aren't anchored down, you can take your heart, and hope, off of Jesus. It's not that they mean any harm, they are just stating the obvious. Faith says Jesus overrides the circumstance, and you must stick with Him until the end, even if you don't see anything happening. Just know He is working. Keep the faith.

This is a moment for Jairus to walk away with his head down in defeat. He came to Jesus, had Jesus coming back with him, and because a lady decided to touch Jesus's clothes and testify, time has run out, and his daughter is dead. Jesus tells Jairus five words to reassure his hope and to let him know he came to the right person at the right time: "Don't be afraid. Only believe" (Mark 5:36).

When they arrive at Jairus's house, there is a loud commotion of people weeping and wailing. This can't be a good sight for Jairus to see, but Jesus is with him. Jesus makes a profound statement about the girl's condition. He says to the people at the house, "Why are you making a commotion and weeping? The child is not dead but asleep" (Mark 5:39). The people responded by laughing at Jesus. This was definitely a sure sign to Jesus they didn't believe in His words or His healing power, and because of that, He sent them all outside, except for Jairus, his wife, Peter, James, and John (Mark 5:37,40).

One thing you must always remember is if you don't have faith in the words or works of Jesus, you will not bear witness to His wonder-working power. Jesus had to speak out against his own hometown and family because they didn't believe in Him: "A prophet is not without honor except in His hometown, among His relatives, and in His household" (Mark 6:4). Because of this, Jesus was not able to do a miracle (Mark 6:5).

When Jesus makes the claim that the little girl is asleep, He isn't saying something to get a reaction out of people. He is speaking this by faith because He believes the Father has already restored the little girl to life. Mark 5:41-42 says, "Then He took the child by the hand and said to her *"Talitha koum"* (which is translated, "Little girl, I say to you, get up"). Immediately the girl got up and began to walk. (She was twelve years old.) At this they were utterly astounded."

Verse 42 reveals something that makes a connection with Jairus and the woman with the issue of blood. It says that the little girl was twelve years old. That means that the woman with the issue of blood had been struggling with her plight for the same length of time that Jairus's daughter had been alive. When Jairus heard the woman say she had been dealing with the issue for twelve years and was immediately healed after her encounter with Jesus, he should have rejoiced and had hope for his daughter that Jesus could deliver her too!

When you read Matthew 5:21-43, what you are seeing is a divine set up by God. God orchestrated for Jairus to come to Jesus and for the woman to show up at the same time. This was all mainly for Jairus's benefit, because even though he came to Jesus, God wanted to put his faith to the test. There are going to be times when you come to God first, but He will make you wait. You will see other people get their prayers answered, and give their testimony, while you are still standing there waiting. God wants to know if we are able to say "hallelujah" for somebody else being blessed while we are on standby. Can we truly be happy for that person, or will we be hurt? God wants to know if we can find hope for our situation through someone else getting healed. Can you praise God because you know He is going to come through for you when it's your time, or will you sit and pout?

Jairus got to Jesus first, but he had to wait. While he was waiting, God was giving him an opportunity to worship through someone else's deliverance. The woman's testimony was providing hope for his own plight. If you are waiting on God to address your plight, keep praying and praising, whether it's your time or not. Be happy for others who come before you. Jesus is still there with you, and He has not forgotten about you. When you don't know what else to do, remember those five reassuring words that Jesus said: "Don't be afraid. Only believe." (Mark 5:36).

As we go into this third passage of Scriptures, one thing we must understand about our calling, or purpose, is that it is tied to something we are passionate about. It might take you a while to realize it, but if you truly pay attention, you will see that what God has purposed for your life matches what you are passionate about. I have a passion for encouraging and uplifting people. I always find joy in letting someone know they can overcome the obstacles, or they can achieve their dreams if they just keep pressing and applying themselves. God took my passion and purposed it for His gospel. I still encourage and uplift people, but now I back it up with Scripture so there is a Biblical source to look back to. I also pray a seed is being planted if they are someone who doesn't know Jesus or doesn't have a strong relationship with Him.

God has also blessed me with the opportunity to write this book because of my purpose and passion. It is my prayer that everyone who reads this book is inspired and uplifted to seek God and to trust Him, no matter how bad things are. He is able to turn your situation around, and this book is my testimony and encouragement to others who might find themselves in similar situations as I was. Or, if you simply don't know Jesus, I pray the words of this book inspire you to seek Him as your Lord and Savior.

When I talk about purpose and passion, the person who comes to mind for me is Peter. Jesus met him in the midst of his passion and turned it into a purpose fit for His kingdom. In Luke Chapter 5, Jesus is preparing to preach to the crowd, but they are pressing in on Him. In order to have room to speak, Jesus gets into a boat that belongs to Peter and asks him to pull out a bit into the sea. Once there, He proceeds to preach to the crowd from the boat (Luke 5:1-3). Jesus finishes preaching to the crowd, and now it's time to have a personal experience with Peter that will change his life forever. Jesus tells Peter, "Put out into deep water and let down your nets for a catch." Peter responds with an excuse instead of expectation. He says, "Master, we have worked hard all night long and caught nothing. But if you say so, I'll let down the nets" (Luke 5:4-5).

The result of Peter letting down the nets turned into an overflow of fish so great, the nets started to tear! Peter had to call for backup in order to haul it all in (Luke 5:6-7)! Peter might have had a moment of doubt, but it quickly turned into a moment of devotion. Peter says to Jesus, "Go away from me, because I am a sinful man, Lord" (Luke 5:8)! Jesus responds by saying, "Don't be afraid. From now on you will be catching people" (Luke 5:10). Your passion is just a passion until Jesus shows up. When Jesus shows up, He magnifies your passion, so it fits the purpose He has placed in you for ministry.

Peter became a faithful disciple unto Jesus, but Peter also had some failures on his journey of faith. Possibly his biggest failure came when he denied Jesus three times. Even worse, Jesus warned Peter he would do it, but Peter didn't believe it: "Simon, Simon, look out. Satan has asked to sift you like wheat. But I have prayed for you that your faith may not fail. And you, when you have turned back, strengthen your brothers" (Luke 22:31-32).

Notice what Jesus is telling Peter. Satan has gained permission from God to trouble Peter. Jesus tells Peter He is praying that his faith doesn't fail. He's letting Peter know he is about to fail, but Jesus wants his faith to remain strong. His faith needs to remain strong because, when he bounces back from his failure, Jesus wants him to strengthen the other disciples.

Peter's response to Jesus is, "Lord, I'm ready to go with you both to prison and to death" (Luke 22:33). Peter is determined to let Jesus know he is the man, and he is ready to endure anything, and anyone, who might come their way. Instead of taking heed to what Jesus has just told him, Peter taps into his pride and has persuaded himself he will not fail his Lord and Savior. Jesus simply tells him one more truth, which would come to fruition within the coming hours: "I tell you, Peter, the rooster will not crow today until you deny three times that you know me" (Luke 22:34).

There are going to be moments on this journey where we feel we are invincible. God has chosen us, we've answered, and His blessings and favor are pouring out left and right. He lets us in on His plans and purposes as we press forward, and we are even presented with the opportunity to be a blessing and a help to others. The power and presence of God is flowing so well that, eventually, we think it's us making things happen.

God takes notice of such things, and when our pride is on display, He will send some pressure our way via Satan. When you are feeling the attacks of the enemy on your life, you can rest assured that God has given him permission to do so. God cannot use us if we are more focused on ourselves and our own efforts. That is stealing glory from Him, and God doesn't share His glory with anyone (Isaiah 42:8). God wants to restore us to a place of humility, so our actions and attitude are holy within His presence.

The time has now come that Jesus has been warning the disciples about. He has been arrested and is being prepared to be handed over to the authorities. Peter, however, is following close by, but fear is about to take precedence over his faith. Imagine the mindset of the disciples right now. They have been following Jesus for three years, and they have witnessed Him do some mighty and miraculous things. They even bore witness to Him speaking to a raging sea storm, and it immediately calmed down (Luke 8:22-25). They are now watching the Messiah be taken captive and escorted away, and He isn't doing anything to stop it. I imagine some of the disciples are worried that maybe Jesus isn't who He has proclaimed to be. If they have taken Jesus captive, then what will be the outcome if they are caught with Him?

Peter is following at a distance. Maybe he's still having a pride moment and wants to show Jesus he is truly a ride or die disciple, or maybe he's waiting to see how Jesus will get Himself out of this situation. What Peter is about to discover is that everything Jesus said to him was true. Luke 22:55-57 says, "They lit a fire in the middle of the courtyard and sat down together, and Peter sat among them. When a servant saw him sitting in the light, and looked closely at him, she said, "This man was with Him too." But he denied it: "Woman, I don't know him." Peter would go on to deny the Lord two more times, but the last time was a gut punch. Luke 22:60b-62 says, "Immediately, while he was still speaking, a rooster crowed. Then the Lord turned and looked at Peter. So, Peter remembered the Word of the Lord, how He had said to him, 'Before the rooster crows today, you will deny me three times.' And he went outside and wept bitterly."

Peter was in a difficult situation. He wanted to show his faith by being present, but his fear of the consequences caused him to deny his Lord and Savior. We must make sure that we take a stand for Jesus in the midst of our calling. There are so many people who are called to ministry, but for the sake of their reputation around family, friends, and co-workers, they will deny Christ. They aren't under the pressure of persecution and death like Peter, but they are under the pressure of remaining critical in the culture, so they don't get cancelled because of their commitment to Christ. Jesus makes it clear in Luke 12:8-9 when He says, "And I say to you, anyone who acknowledges Me before others, the Son of Man will also acknowledge him before the angels of God, but whoever denies Me before others will be denied before the angels of God."

Peter isn't the only person to fail Jesus, and he certainly will not be the last. When we fail God, it leaves us feeling defeated and unworthy of the calling God has placed within us. It's easy to give up and just walk away or go into hiding, especially if your failure has produced public shame. When we show God that we are sincerely regretful of our mistake, He is willing to restore and renew us because our passion and purpose still has promise. When we seek restoration, sometimes God will take us back to our moment of failure. It's not meant to remind us of the pain, but it's a moment to repent of the sin that was committed, request God's forgiveness, and to be released from the pain and guilt that has us bound. God is giving us the opportunity to overcome the failure so that it no longer overrules us.

Peter is in a place of sorrow. Everything Jesus said he would do, he did it. Jesus has also been crucified and buried. Peter is sorrowful because he truly thought he would never forsake Jesus the way he did. Have you ever been there? It's not a good feeling when you do something that displeases the Lord, especially something you thought you would never do. The guilt, pain, and disappointment possibly has Peter feeling he is no longer worthy of his calling. John 21:2-3a says, "Simon Peter, Thomas (called "Twin"), Nathanael from Cana of Galilee, Zebedee's sons, and two other of His disciples were together. "I'm going fishing," Simon Peter said to them. "We're coming with you."

What Peter is truly saying is that he quits. He's no longer worthy of the ministry or leading the other disciples. He's giving it all up, and he's heading back to what he used to do. He's going fishing, and the other disciples are following suit. The easiest thing to do after you have failed is to quit. The embarrassment, guilt, and shame of your mistake can make you want to crawl into a hole and stay there. What you don't realize is there are people watching how you handle the fallout. They want to see if you're going to quit or find a way to get back on your quest to serve the Lord. Notice when Peter said he was going fishing, the other disciples decided to join him. They saw Peter was giving up on the ministry, so they decided they would too.

Peter has returned to his life before Christ. He's gone back to his passion, but he's doing it with no purpose. Some people return back to their old ways of living when a failure happens. They return to the alcohol, drugs, weed, pornography, and the night clubs. These things used to be a passion for them, but now, it has no purpose. It's simply a way to avoid having to deal with the elephant in the room: their failure. Peter and the other disciples have returned to an old way of living but there is nothing available for them. John 21:3b says, "They went out and got into the boat but that night they caught nothing."

God will let you go back to what you used to do, but you will discover how empty it is because you are used to the fullness of Christ fulfilling every aspect of your life. He won't let you dwell in that dead situation for long though. He loves you, and He still has a plan and a purpose for you to fulfill. God wants to restore you unto Himself, and He wants to reconcile the situation.

Peter still has a calling on his life to fulfill and Jesus wasn't going to let him off the hook that easy. Jesus is about to do two things with Peter: He's going to take him back to a familiar moment that caused him to believe, and then He is going to take him back to the failing moment when Peter denied Him three times.

Peter and the disciples have been out fishing all night, and they haven't caught anything. Suddenly, they have an encounter with Jesus, but they aren't aware it is Him. John 21:4-5 says, "When daybreak came, Jesus stood on the shore, but the disciples did not know it was Jesus. "Friends," Jesus called to them, "you don't have any fish, do you?" "No," they answered.

Notice that Jesus calls them "friends." Peter denied Jesus three times, and the other disciples were nowhere to be found when He was taken away to be crucified. Yet, He calls them His friends. I believe we can be honest here and say if our close friends would have done these things, we would no longer be calling them our friends. We probably wouldn't even want to deal with them anymore because, in our time of need, they left us to suffer alone.

The love and compassion Jesus has for us is beyond our comprehension. Its unconditional love, which means He loves us in spite of who we are and what we have done. The beautiful thing about the love of Christ is there is nothing you can do to cause Him to stop loving you. He is still your friend, even after your failure and after everyone else has left you. Jesus is still there waiting to restore the fellowship and to renew your commitment to the call that He has given you.

In John 21:6, Jesus says to them, "Cast the net on the right side of the boat and you'll find some." So, they did, and they were unable to haul it in because of the large number of fish. This is a replay of what Jesus did in Luke Chapter 5 when He told Peter to pull out into the water and let down his net. It is a moment Jesus is providing which reminds Peter and the disciples of that great miracle, and it also reveals who the man is on the shore that has told them to do this. "The disciple, the one Jesus loved, said to Peter, "It is the Lord" (John 21:7a)! This causes Peter to put his clothes back on, jump out the boat, and swim to the shore! The other disciples came in the boat with all of the fish they had caught (John 21:7b-8).

When you go away from Jesus because of your disappointment and failure, He will show up and do something that causes you to remember Him and the goodness He poured into your life. When you remember, you will recognize it is Him drawing you out of your dark place and back into His presence. Run to Him and be restored!

Peter has rushed back to be by the Lord's side. Can you imagine how Peter is feeling right now? He must be rejoicing with greatness that Jesus is alive and well, but at the same time, there must be a feeling of remorse and regret for what he did. He knows that Jesus has not forgotten about it. What will Jesus say to him? What will Jesus do to him? Will Jesus cast him out from being a disciple? Not at all. Jesus wants to restore Peter, but He must return Peter to the familiar and painful place where he failed.

John 21:9-12 says, *"When they got out on land, they saw a charcoal fire there, with fish lying on it, and bread. "Bring some of the fish you've just caught," Jesus told them. So, Simon Peter climbed up and hauled the net ashore, full of large fish-153 of them. Even though there were so many, the net was not torn. "Come and have breakfast," Jesus told them. None of the disciples dared ask Him, 'Who are you?' because they knew it was the Lord."*

Jesus is setting up a powerful restoration session for Peter. Notice there is a charcoal fire. Guess where Peter was when he denied Jesus three times? He was around a charcoal fire (Luke 22:55; John 18:18). Jesus invites them to have breakfast. It's been a long night of fishing and three days of sadness and sorrow. The disciples knew they were with the Lord again, but this occasion is specifically for Peter. Peter denied Jesus three times around a charcoal fire, but Jesus is going to restore Peter three times around His charcoal fire.

"When they had eaten breakfast, Jesus asked Simon Peter, "Simon, son of John, do you love Me more than these?" "Yes, Lord," he said to Him, "You know that I love You." "Feed My lambs," He told him (John 21:15).

Why would Jesus ask Peter this question? Because Peter once proclaimed his love for Jesus was greater than that of the other disciples (Matthew 26:31-33). Peter is in a humble place now and will not make such a proclamation after the failure he displayed. He is in a proper place where Jesus can use him for ministry. When we return to Jesus after a failure, we should be in a humble place. Our failure should have knocked us down a few notches, and Jesus should be the only one who lifts us back up. Matthew 23:12 says, "Whoever exalts himself will be humbled, and whoever humbles himself will be exalted." Keep your head low, and let Jesus take you higher.

Jesus wasn't finished yet. He came to Peter a second time and said, "Simon, son of John, do you love Me?" "Yes, Lord," he said to Him, "You know that I love You." "Shepherd My sheep," He told him (John 21:16). Jesus was calling Peter to lead the people in a godly manner and to be an example to the flock of what a Christian should look like. Jesus wants us to get back in the game because there is work to do for the kingdom. He is challenging us to lead with sincerity and according to the truth of His Word. Our failure should become a testimony to others that Jesus is able to restore and renew our lives, no matter how far we have fallen.

He asked him the third time, "Simon, son of John, do you love Me?" Peter was grieved He asked him the third time, "Do you love Me?" He said, "Lord, You know everything; You know that I love You." "Feed My sheep," Jesus said (John 21:17).

Jesus wanted to make sure Peter took his restoration and his calling to heart. We would all be like Peter if we stood before Jesus and He asked us three times if we loved Him. It would make us feel as if we did something so offensive, that He's trying to make sure our love for Him is real. Jesus is letting Peter know that yes, he hurt Him, but He isn't holding it over his head. He is restoring the fellowship, and He wants Peter to know the call on his life is vital.

Jesus wants us to know we have the power to overcome the odds and failures, and above all, to forgive ourselves because He has forgiven us. Get ready to get back in the game! Jesus has called you to a place and a purpose, and His restoration will equip you to be better and to do better than you did before.

Peter took his restoration and his call to heart. He is now in a place where Jesus can use him in full measure. Before Jesus ascended back to heaven, he told the disciples, "But you will receive power when the Holy Spirt has come on you, and you will be My witnesses in Jerusalem, in all Judea and Samaria, and to the end of the earth" (Acts 1:8). Peter experienced this power from the Holy Spirit and it caused him to go forth and do a great work for the kingdom of God and for the church.

When it came time to choose a replacement for Judas, it was Peter who stood up and spoke about the matter (Acts 1:15-26). On the day of Pentecost, the Holy Spirit came upon Peter and everyone who was assembled in the room (Acts 2:1-4). After being accused of being drunk by outside witnesses, Peter preached his first sermon, which lead to about 3,000 people being saved (Acts 2:13-41).

It was Peter who told the lame man "I don't have silver or gold, but what I do have, I give you: In the name of Jesus Christ of Nazareth, get up and walk" (Acts 3:6)! When Peter preached his second sermon, about 5,000 people were saved (Acts 3:11-4:4). It was Peter who stood before the Jewish rulers and proclaimed the lame man's healing came through the power of the name of Jesus Christ. Peter concluded his message by letting them know, "There is salvation in no one else, for there is no other name under heaven given to people by which we must be saved" (Acts 4:12).

Through the power of the Holy Spirit, it was Peter who confronted Ananias and his wife, Sapphira, for lying to the Holy Spirit, which resulted in both of them dying (Acts 5:1-11).

After being restored into fellowship with Jesus, Peter's failure couldn't compare to the fulfillment of ministry that the Holy Spirit caused him to do. Peter went from denying Christ to demanding Christ be the one and only Savior of all! God is able to turn your life around and to elevate you beyond any level you could ever imagine. If you have failed in your ministry, marriage, money, or morality, please return to Jesus, repent of your sins, and watch Him renew your heart and mind to do better and to go boldly for the gospel and the kingdom of God.

THE CONCLUSION

Proverbs 16:3 says, "Commit your activities to the LORD, and your plans will be established." Writing this book was a two-year journey, and I thank God for the experience and for choosing me to be the author. I had it in my head that I wanted to write a book. The thought went from my head to my heart. Writing a book was something I seriously wanted to do. I took what was in my heart and placed it into God's hands, and I asked Him to cultivate it. He responded by giving me the title of this book, and He also gave me the titles of the chapters.

I responded by faith by going out and buying a laptop. I typed up the cover page, the dedication page, and the table of contents with no problem. When I got ready to start my introduction, I asked God, "What do I write?" He told me to just start writing. When I started writing, He poured out words, wisdom, ideas, and Scriptures. He gave me everything I needed to complete this book.

This book is not only my testimony of how God took my failure and turned it into something fruitful. It is also a book that provides strength and encouragement for anyone who has walked away from God or is trying to figure out life, but only coming up with failing results. My prayer is that this book reminds you of who God is, and it causes you to remember the wonderful things He has done in your life. It's not too late to turn around. Go back to Him and let Him give you a second chance to do things right and according to His will and His way.

If you have read this book and you do not know Jesus or have reservations about accepting Him as your Lord and Savior, I pray something was written in this book that will cause you to truly seek Him and accept Him. Jesus loves you, and He died for your sins, so you don't have to make that payment. John 10:9-10 says, "I am the gate. If anyone enters by Me, he will be saved and will come in and go out and find pasture. A thief only comes to steal and kill and destroy. I have come so that they may have life and have it in abundance." Don't let the devil deceive you into believing that your life is good without God. Place your trust in Jesus Christ today and experience the greatness of His love for you both now and in eternity.

I have learned so much from writing this book. Studying Jonah has really opened up a window to really see myself and to recognize that there is always something about us that needs God's work. I'm learning to follow His Word and His will, even if it is something I'm truly not interested in doing. I understand it isn't about me or how I feel. God wants to make an impact in someone's life, and it might come at the cost of me being inconvenienced. It gives me the opportunity to submit to Him so He can use me and fulfill His plans without my personal thoughts and feelings getting in the way.

I'm happy to testify that during the writing of this book, Tonia and I received some wonderful blessings from God. He provided me the opportunity to attend Asbury Theological Seminary, where I finished with a master's in biblical and theological foundations. He also increased the number of our household. On November 14, 2022, we welcomed our second son, Micah, into our family! Jeremiah loves being a big brother, and I thank God each and every day for my wife and my boys. God is still moving and shifting the atmosphere, so I am excited to see what plans and opportunities are coming our way!

Thank you again for purchasing this book. I thank God for taking a simple thought and turning it into something tangible that people can touch.

"How happy is the one who does not walk in the advice of the wicked or stand in the pathway with sinners or sit in the company of mockers! Instead, his delight is in the LORD's instruction, and he meditates on it day and night. He is like a tree planted beside flowing streams that bears its fruit in its season and whose leaf does not wither. Whatever he does prospers" Psalm 1:1-3.

www.ingramcontent.com/pod-product-compliance
Lightning Source LLC
Chambersburg PA
CBHW051431090426
42737CB00014B/2924